D0944154

THE
REFORMING
POWER
OF THE
SCRIPTURES

~

A BIOGRAPHY OF THE ENGLISH BIBLE

THE REFORMING POWER OF THE SCRIPTURES

A BIOGRAPHY OF THE ENGLISH BIBLE

Mary Metzner Trammell & William G. Dawley

The Christian Science Publishing Society

BOSTON

Publisher's Cataloging in Publication
(Prepared by Quality Books Inc.)

Trammell, Mary Metzner.
    The reforming power of the scriptures: a biography of the
English Bible / Mary Metzner Trammell & William G. Dawley.
    p. cm.
    Includes bibliographical references.
    Preassigned LCCN: 96-86014
    ISBN 0-87510-314-6

    1. Bible–History. 2. Bible–English–Versions–History.
I. Dawley, William G. II. Title.

BS445.T73 1996   220'.09
                        QBI96-40222

Contents

Foreword

One of the most frequently used icebreakers at social gatherings is the question, "If you were marooned on a desert island and had only one book with you, which one would you want it to be?" A researcher once reported that a staggering number of people answer, "The Bible." And many of them are not even religious believers!

I expect that the castaways who want it with them on their islands have different reasons for their choice. For most people, the most important reason is that they believe the Bible to be the reliable record of God's dealings with His people over the centuries. They believe it is the very Word of God from which the way of life and worship expected of them is derived. Its writings are inspired as well as instructive, and people's lives find illumination, guidance, nourishment, and healing in its pages.

This "biography" of the Bible is a fascinating story. Full of divine wonder and awe, it is also a tale of human mystery and drama, suffering and joy, heroism and devotion, irony and humor. It is, above all, a life story that presents us at every turn with a deep sense of God's everlasting care for His people, and His people's flawed but persistent desire to be faithful. It is a majestic story that deserves a good telling by able tellers. And in this volume, we have just that!

Even for many other people, who may not hold the stories and teachings of the Bible to be the authentic Word of God, the Bible is still a great human document, full of beauty, wisdom, and power. For still others, the Bible has value because it has profoundly shaped the culture in which we live. It has immense importance as a work of literature. They love its memorable words and stories, its lofty principles and values, its fertile ideas and images—as a book of books, a library of poetry, chronicle, story, history, and law. People hold it in high regard for the way it shapes the human imagination.

Regardless of their reasons for wanting to have a Bible with them, our castaways would easily be able to get their wish to have one. Today the Scriptures are the most widely published and widely read texts in history. Bibles are everywhere, in thousands of different versions and translations.

This easy access was not always the case. The story of the Hebrew and Christian Bible—how it came to be written in the first place, the different books it contains, the many translations that were made into various languages from its authors' original tongues—is also the story of people's struggle to obtain and use freely the Word at the center of their lives.

At times, the Bible was actually a dangerous book. In the era when the Old Testament Book of Daniel was written, for example, Jews who were found reading the Scriptures (Torah) could be put to death by the enemies of their faith! In the history of Christianity, the Bible was at times forbidden to the people also, not by enemies, but by the very leaders of the church. They believed that, unless properly interpreted, the Bible could mislead and misinform people as easily as it could inspire them to the good. Thus, in their zeal for correct interpretation, they sometimes made the Scriptures seem like something to be feared and avoided more than pored over and loved.

Yet desire for God's Word never diminished, and the Christian people's need for it eventually won out. Therefore, the Bible's story is also about the power of the Scriptures to form and re-form the Christian Church. Century after century, the return to its pages has been one all-important source of new life, light, and healing for Christians.

Sometimes this new light was shed gently over the church, but at other times it broke forth only by painful revolutions. After many generations of struggle, today even the churches that once forbade the reading of the Scriptures by "ordinary people" in their native tongue encourage and support the daily reading of God's Word. Thankfully, nowadays the Bible's reforming power is available to anyone who seeks it, even on a desert isle!

From different backgrounds and perspectives, the authors, Mary Trammell and William Dawley, have dedicated their lives to teaching and researching this story. The book you have in your hands represents a vast knowledge distilled into a few pages. But it also represents a deep love for the Scriptures and the conviction that knowing them can have a transforming effect on our lives. It is that love and that conviction, even more than the erudition and vivid writing, that make the story told here come fully alive.

The authors aim to educate us about the Bible's origins, its many forms over the centuries, its heroic translators, teachers, and defenders. Their hope is to stimulate our reverence for God's Word and to increase our desire to know and be healed by its wisdom. Their achievement is to have accomplished both with admirable skill and even more admirable devotion.

May we read their words to be informed—but even more, may everything we read in these chapters draw us to the Bible itself, to be refreshed, reformed, and strengthened for the life of faith and for faithful service.

J. Mary Luti
Associate Dean
Andover Newton Theological Seminary

Acknowledgments

We want to thank The Christian Science Board of Directors, the Board of Trustees of The Christian Science Publishing Society, and the Editor of the Christian Science periodicals, William F. Moody, for giving us the opportunity to write *The Reforming Power of the Scriptures.* Without their encouragement and support, the series in *The Christian Science Journal,* and this book, could never have happened. We thank them for believing in this project, and for giving us both the time and the free rein to work on it. We're grateful, too, for our capable reviewers: Dr. Brook Ballard, Professor Emeritus of History at Principia College, and Dr. Mary J. Luti, Associate Dean at Andover Newton Theological Seminary.

In 1992 we began work on "The Reforming Power of the Scriptures," a monthly series that appeared for approximately two years—between 1992 and 1994—in *The Christian Science Journal.* The series showed the Judeo-Christian Bible as part of an even wider tapestry of Scripture—as the revelation of God's Word in the world's great religions and philosophies. The work continued Dr. Trammell's long research in Bible history.

Mary Metzner Trammell, Ph. D.
William G. Dawley
Boston

I
INTRODUCTION

CHAPTER ONE

The World's Scriptures from Cave Dwellers to Christianity

E ven before the beginning of recorded history, men and women have had a desire to document their innermost spiritual feelings— to *share* them with others, even to help change, or reform, the lives of those around them. People have expressed these feelings in a number of ways—through pictures, symbols, verbal communication, and written language. You might say that, in a very broad sense, the word *scripture* includes all of these expressions.

The earliest traces of humanity's spiritual outreach show up in paintings on the walls of caves in what is now Europe. For example, in the Pyrenees Mountains of southern France, deep within a cave known as Trois Frères, an eerie figure has stared at onlookers for some thirty thousand years. His dark, compelling eyes peer out through the mask of a stag with antlers. Scholars tell us that this figure represents a shaman—a priest or medicine man of primitive cultures.

Animal and nature worship continued for thousands of years in tribelike societies that grew out of Ice Age communities and spread worldwide. Before Europeans set foot upon the Americas, for instance, more than two thousand Indian tribes with different languages and cultures populated these vast continents, with the shaman retaining his position at the spiritual center of the tribe. Ceremonial prayers and traditions were passed down from generation to generation, but none were recorded in holy books. Instead they were depicted on animal skins, as well as in chants, drumbeating, music, and dance.

Painting of the "Sorcerer" in the cave of Les Trois Frères, France

EARLY MEDITERRANEAN SCRIPTURES

In the Nile River delta around twenty-six hundred years before the birth of Jesus Christ, the Egyptians painted and carved their religious beliefs on the walls of mammoth pyramids and molded colossal stone sphinxes. Like the early tribal peoples, they worshiped part-person, part-animal beings. They also worshiped other types of deities—such

3

as river crocodiles, birds, and cats. And they revered humanlike gods and goddesses representing the forces of nature—rain, fire, earth, water—and deities representing the full range of mortal emotions.

King worship also played a major role in early Egyptian religious beliefs. These people called their kings, who they believed were descended from the gods, pharaohs. In fact, they saw their pharaohs as incarnations of the god Horus, who usually appeared in human form with the head of a falcon.

Several hundred miles to the north across the Mediterranean, another ancient society was developing—the Minoans on the island of Crete. There, according to Greek mythology, the legendary King Minos, after whom the civilization was named, was said to have married the goddess Pasiphaë, the daughter of the sun. Their monstrous child, the bloodthirsty Minotaur, consumed young men and women sacrificed to him by the island people. Eventually, the Minotaur was slain in a labyrinth by the hero Theseus. In this early agricultural society, a fertility goddess became another central figure worshiped by the people.

With the advent of the Bronze Age, the Cretans' worship and scripture became more sophisticated. The borrowed Greek Minotaur myth was literally cast in stone in the "Labyrinth," an enormous palace that covered six acres and was built for one of the priest-kings reigning at the high point of the Minoan civilization. When these king-gods invaded the Greek mainland, Cretan culture and religion swept over the Greek city-states.

As the centuries progressed, the Greek deities became more sophisticated and humanlike—turning into the urbane, courtly, and often unpredictable set of characters we meet in Homer's great eighth-century B.C. epics: the *Iliad* and the *Odyssey*. It's these splendid poetic epics about the Greeks' glorious victory in the Trojan War that in a sense constitute the sacred writings of the Greek people.

The closest thing to a full theological statement of Greek myth was written by Hesiod in about 800 B.C. Combining traditional Greek gods and goddesses with Oriental myths, Hesiod described in his book *Theogony* an array of deities around Gaea (the Earth) and Uranus (the Heavens). And he told how Moira (Fate) had the upper hand over these gods and spirits, always surprising them with some new turn of events.

In the fifth century B.C., during the Age of Pericles (the states-man who helped launch democracy in Athens), the Greek religion became more and more man-centered. The philosopher Socrates—who asked Athenians penetrating questions about soul and body, and about the real and the ideal—became the key intellectual force in Greece. His student Plato founded an academy to perpetuate Socrates' teachings and wrote down most of what his master said in a collection of dialogues that weren't religious scriptures in the strict sense of the word but did hint at the spirituality of man and the universe.

About this same time, a vigorous new culture was slowly building in what is now Italy. The burgeoning republic of Rome became an aggressive military power that took over the Greek city-states one by one. As this happened, the Romans inevitably adopted most of the Greek gods and goddesses, giving them new Latin names.

In the last centuries before the birth of Jesus, mythology became less and less important to both the Greeks and the Romans. And the ever-enlarging Roman Empire became a type of religion in its own right—with Julius Caesar's *Commentaries* on Rome's conquest of Gaul serving as a kind of "scripture" celebrating this civic religion.

THE JUDEO-CHRISTIAN SCRIPTURES

As these various forms of worship and scripture were developing in Greece and Rome, a very different religious way of life was taking shape in the Middle East. In the eighteenth century B.C., in what is now southern Iraq (then known as Mesopotamia), a man named Abram—the leader of a tribe of gypsylike desert wanderers—came face to face with a radically new concept of God. This God, whom he called Yahweh, talked with Abram. Instinctively, Abram believed Yahweh's words and acted according to His commands. In this area of the world, known as the Fertile Crescent because of its rich soil, Abram's ideas about Yahweh were revolutionary. Men and women of the predominant Amorite culture worshiped personal gods, fertility gods, and king-gods. Each individual prayed to his own deity.

But at the age of seventy-five, Abram, in obedience to Yahweh's direction, gathered his family and herds together and led them southward to the land of Canaan, part of which is known today as Israel. Here, Yahweh made an agreement with Abram called a "covenant." The terms of this agreement were that Abram and his children would

Where the Tigris and Euphrates rivers meet in the Fertile Crescent

always follow and obey Yahweh. In turn, Yahweh promised to protect and care for Abram's family and descendants. He promised to give Abram and his children the land of Canaan "for an everlasting possession." And because of Abram's faithfulness, Yahweh renamed him Abraham, or "Father of Many People."

Over the years the account of Abraham's covenant with Yahweh passed from parent to child, from generation to generation. Gradually a tradition began to take shape—one that inspired these early Apiru, or Hebrew, people to love and follow their God wherever He might lead them. When Abraham's grandson Jacob discovered Yahweh for himself, God gave him a new name—Israel. From then on, all of Jacob's descendants were known as the children of Israel. Knowing that they were Yahweh's own people gave the Hebrews courage to remain true to their God, even when Egypt enslaved them several centuries later.

About five hundred years after Abraham, a dynamic leader named Moses emerged among the children of Israel in Egypt. He encouraged his people to revolt against the pharaoh-god of Egypt and led Abraham's descendants across the Red Sea, into the Arabian desert, and on toward Canaan. On the way, Yahweh revealed to Moses in tablets of stone the first written scripture of the Hebrew people—the Ten Commandments.

These Commandments gave the people a law to live by, requiring in no uncertain terms that the children of Israel worship Yahweh alone, pray to Him, and rest on His holy day. But the Commandments also told the Hebrews how to treat each other: to obey their parents and to refrain from killing, stealing, lying, and committing adultery. The Commandments made it clear that Yahweh is an entirely spiritual God, not to be likened to any material thing in heaven or on earth. No images or animals or human beings could possibly represent His majesty and might. And Yahweh knows no limits and is bound to no specific place; He *moved* with His people as they wandered from oasis to oasis, from landmark to landmark, in their laborious journey back to Canaan.

Out of the original Ten Commandments, which were revealed to Moses on Mount Sinai, grew the entire body of oral Hebrew teachings, some blended with the earlier Sumerian and Amorite scriptures of the Middle East. There was a collection of psalms praising Yahweh; a collection of wise sayings, or proverbs; a body of laws on virtually every aspect of eating, living, and working; a full history of early tribal leaders, known as patriarchs; and the story of a long-suffering but faithful man named Job.

In song and ritual story—around campfires in the desert night or later in the resettled villages of Canaan—the children of Israel told and retold the ancient history about their beginnings, their genesis as a people. Sometime around 1000 B.C., this body of Scripture evolved into the first five books of the Hebrew Bible, known as the Pentateuch (the law according to Moses and his followers). And later came the rest of the Hebrew Bible—vibrant with the ringing words of the great Hebrew prophets, holy men who wouldn't let the Jewish people forget their covenant (or testament) with Yahweh and who foretold the coming of a Messiah, or Saviour, for the Israelites if they remained true to their God.

Over the centuries, the Pentateuch became known as the Torah. And, as the body of Hebrew Scripture developed to include doctrine, prophecy, psalms, proverbs, and so on, people often used the term *Torah* to describe the entire "Old Testament."

In time, literally every child, including the young prophet Jesus of Nazareth, learned about these Scriptures, could quote from them, and loved them. But Jesus and his followers, who believed he was the promised Messiah, would make a new covenant with God—a "new testament" based on universal love. They preached the "gospel," or good news, of this new covenant not only in Israel but throughout the Greek and Roman world, where they won large numbers of converts to their way of life and established a vigorous new religion known as Christianity. The account of Jesus' lifework and of the founding of the Christian Church is an extension of the Hebrew Bible and is known as the New Testament.

SCRIPTURES OF THE EAST

Parallel to the evolution of the Hebrew and Christian Scriptures in the Middle East, another major religious tradition was slowly building in the Far East. Some twenty-five hundred years before the birth of Jesus, a highly advanced civilization established itself in the Indus Valley of what is now India. The people of this early society revered nature gods.

Then about 1750 B.C. a warlike northern European people swept through the Khyber Pass. These conquerors mingled with the indigenous people of the Indus Valley, imposed their tribal religious beliefs on them, and gradually developed a new "Hindu" culture. And out of the poetic hymns that these North Europeans brought with them into their new homeland grew the first scriptures of the "Hindu people."

Over the next thousand years in India, the entire body of Vedic, or Hindu, scripture evolved. (*Veda* means "knowledge.") These sacred writings began with what is called the *Rigveda,* a collection of more than a thousand poems and hymns dedicated to the many nature gods the North European people believed in. From the *Rigveda,* several other types of scripture came into being—theological and ritual commentaries, instructions for sacrifices, verses set to music, magic formulas, prayers to cure disease and cast out demons, and even love charms.

Then, in the sixth century B.C., a man named Siddhartha Gautama, who came to be known as Buddha (or the Enlightened One), renounced a life of luxury and ease in his enormous palace and began a single-minded search for truth. Years later Siddhartha achieved what he called total enlightenment. In compassion for humanity, he shared his revelations in his great Deer Park Sermon, a summary of the truth that had been revealed to him.

The teachings of this sermon—together with an enormous number of rules for living, aphorisms called "sutras," and details about Buddha's life—were gathered over the years into several Sanskrit collections, or canons. The most famous of these collections, the Pali Canon of Ceylon and Southeast Asia, is the primary written scripture of the Buddhist religion.

In Persia, meanwhile, another key religion started developing in the seventh century B.C. This movement began humbly in the wilds of Mount Alburz, where a teenage prophet named Zoroaster retreated for almost fifteen years to a cave. There he spent his time in meditation, until he received a vision of a supreme Lord, whom he called

Ahura Mazda. After this revelation, he summarized Mazda's message in poems or hymns that brought out three great standards of human conduct: Purity, Uprightness, and Truth. These hymns (or Gathas) explain that there are two basic powers—good (Asha) and evil (Druj)—and that humanity has to choose between them. Eventually, Zoroaster's writings and those of his followers were collected in the body of Persian scripture called the *Avesta.*

A century later in China, a gentle reformer named Lao-tzu, or "Old Master," preached his beliefs. A hermit who hid away in a mountain hut most of his life, Lao-tzu felt *all* people are capable of understanding truth, of becoming the "Master." *Tao,* meaning "The Way," is at the very center of his teachings. A compilation of brief proverbs or sayings constitutes the scripture of Lao-tzu's followers, who are called Taoists.

Confucius, a member of the royal court, was a younger contemporary of Lao-tzu in China. Said to have been more than nine feet tall, Confucius rested all of his faith in the traditional wisdom of antiquity. He collected and expounded upon ideas of the past in six books, which he edited rather than wrote. To Confucius, the highest virtue was obedience to parents and to rulers of the state. His *Tao* was a sort of middle way, dedicated to virtues like faithfulness, wisdom, righteousness, generosity, and strict decorum. His was not a religion, strictly speaking, but a complete ethical and philosophical system to live by.

The pre-Christian religions we've surveyed in this chapter literally encircle the earth. They run full circle also in terms of the forms of scripture they produced—ranging from face paint and statuettes to full-blown statements of theology. But the common thread that unites these forms of scripture is the inborn desire men, women, and children have felt since the Stone Age—the desire to worship divinity, to provide direction and purpose for human experience, and to reform lives. In virtually every culture of history, that desire has fired humankind to seek answers to questions people are still asking today: questions like Who am I? Why am I here? Who created me? What maintains my life? How can I be a better man or woman? Various answers to these questions have been recorded and passed on from generation to generation as "scriptures"—the scriptures of the world.

II

EVOLUTION
OF THE
HEBREW
BIBLE

~

The Old Testament: A Love Story between God and His People

In many ways it was like a marriage. There were promises—covenants, as they called them. And a sheer determination to make the marriage work—to make it last forever. Yet this particular marriage was like no other; it was the marriage of God and His people—of the Hebrew God Yahweh and the children of Israel. You might say that the Hebrew Bible, the Old Testament, provides the recorded history of this ancient marriage. It traces the love story between Israel and her God, a story that continues today in the lives of all those who look to the Holy Scriptures for inspiration, peace, and guidance.

THE FIRST COVENANT

The Old Testament could be described as the written story of the making, breaking, and renewal of God's love covenant with His people. Of course, the first holy man to make a covenant with God was Abraham, the father of the Hebrew nation. Literally transformed by his encounter with God, he taught his family to love and follow the God who had appeared to him years earlier.

For generations, Abraham's tribe passed down by word of mouth the story of their family's mutual promise and commitment to God. But the covenant with God was all but forgotten by the time Abraham's descendants migrated to Egypt to save themselves from starvation. In Egypt, as in Canaan, they were tempted to be unfaithful to the God of Abraham—to worship instead local fertility gods and the pharaoh king-god. Eventually enslaved and oppressed by the Egyptians, the Israelites longed to be reunited with their God and to return home as a free people.

THE EXODUS FROM EGYPT AND THE
SINAI COVENANT

As would happen time and again in Israelite history when covenant promises were broken and situations became desperate, a new leader arose to remind the Jewish people of their promises to God through the establishment of a new covenant. The leader who appeared in the thirteenth century B.C. was Moses.

With the pharaoh's troops thundering behind him, Moses boldly led thousands of his people out of Egyptian captivity toward the Red Sea. There, in a wondrous rescue that would become part of the Scriptural tradition of the Hebrew people forever, Yahweh divided the waters and led His people to safety before the Red Sea closed over the heads of the Egyptian troops.

In the wake of this unforgettable release from bondage, the children of Israel moved forward with new confidence that Yahweh truly loved them and that they were His special people. Yet as they slowly trekked through the arid Sinai Desert, short on both food and water, they began to doubt whether God would continue to care for them. As their doubts grew stronger and their complaints more intense, they challenged, almost daily, Moses' ability to lead them.

Just as it seemed the people had lost faith altogether, Yahweh gave them clear signs of His continuing presence. Sweet and delicious manna appeared every morning. And flocks of quail periodically descended in the desert and provided food for the hungry Israelites. Then, when they finally arrived at the oasis of Sinai, came the most momentous sign of all—the appearance of Yahweh Himself in their midst. And with Yahweh's appearance came His Ten Commandments, the divine laws by which the Hebrew people were to rule their lives. Moses also presented a full body of more specific rules for living—known to later generations as simply "the Law." Of all these rules and laws, only the Commandments were written down—inscribed by Yahweh Himself on tablets of stone.

The rest of the Law was remembered solely in the *hearts* of the people, who sometimes obeyed the requirements of the Law, sometimes rebelled against them, but always repeated them faithfully to their children generation after generation—until the Law was finally written down, along with the rest of the Exodus story, over three centuries later.

In a solemn ceremony celebrated by a quiet meal on or near
Mount Sinai, Yahweh sealed a new covenant with His people–
speaking directly to Moses as their representative. It was, in a sense,
a marriage covenant, showing Yahweh's unending devotion to His
people and His promise of all good things to come.

THE PROMISED LAND AND THE
COVENANT AT SHECHEM

After their desert wanderings in the Sinai and the death of Moses
about 1250 B.C.–and in sight of the Promised Land–Joshua became the
military and spiritual leader of the Hebrew people. Convinced that
Yahweh was fighting alongside them on the battlefield, they employed
guerrilla tactics to conquer the land west of the Jordan River, the
southern hills, and finally the northern hill country of Canaan.

Basking in the glow of their brilliant victories over the sophisticated Canaanite people, whom they had all but exterminated, the
Hebrews quickly began to take on the customs, and even the *religion,*
of the Canaanites. Angered, Joshua summoned the twelve tribes of
Israel to a momentous meeting at Shechem. There the fiery leader laid
down an ultimatum to his people. It was time, he said, to make an all-
out commitment to Yahweh. He reminded them of all

*Sketch of a street scene in
Shechem, 1875*

that Yahweh had done for them–delivering them from
bondage in Egypt and giving them a decisive victory in
Canaan. Yet, after all these blessings, the people were
prostituting themselves by adopting the fertility gods
of the Canaanite people. This practice could continue
no longer.

Joshua demanded that the Hebrews make an
immediate choice: worship the one true God or be led
into doom and destruction by false gods. The people did
not hesitate–they chose to wed themselves to Yahweh
forever. So the covenant that the Hebrew people made
with Yahweh at Sinai was renewed at Shechem, but
with a whole new dimension–a fresh commitment literally to live the Law in their new land within a theocratic
community of faith, a Tribal Confederacy that would
fulfill Abraham's vision for his descendants.

From the time of Moses through the Tribal Confederacy, the elements of this faith were transmitted orally, in the form of stories, hymns, prophetic oracles, poetry, and the wise sayings known as proverbs. Although the art of writing had been practiced in the Fertile Crescent as early as 2000 B.C. these oral traditions weren't written down until later.

The poetic psalms clearly sprang from deep feelings toward Yahweh. There were hymns of exultant praise, laments that reached out to Yahweh from the depths of despair, and songs expressing the pure joy of life in Yahweh's courts. There were caustic aphorisms chiding the Israelites for their rebellion against God and long adventure stories—or sagas—celebrating the heroic deeds of the Hebrew patriarchs. And there were thousands of narratives—stories about creation, primeval history, and ritual and cultic practices of the Hebrews. Where did these stories come from? From both Hebrew and non-Hebrew sources, from as far away as ancient Mesopotamia and as close by as the rich mythical tradition of the local Canaanites.

THE COVENANT WITH KING DAVID

We learn from the Old Testament that Israel struggled long against marauding attacks from without and the allurements of Baal worship from within. (Baal was the Canaanite weather god.) Recognizing the need for stability and acting on his authority as spiritual leader of his people, an eleventh-century B.C. Hebrew judge named Samuel appointed and consecrated the first king of Israel, a passionately devoted servant of Yahweh named Saul. Endowed by Yahweh with the charismatic spirit of leadership, Saul led his countrymen in an all-out resistance to the greatest military threat facing them at that time—the Philistines. These seafaring people had terrorized the area around the Aegean Sea for years and were determined to capture the whole eastern Mediterranean as part of their ever-growing empire. Although Saul was at first successful in thwarting the Philistine invasion, he later developed emotional problems that discredited him in the eyes of his people. It was clear to all and especially to Samuel, Saul's spiritual adviser, that the special charisma had departed from Saul.

As it became apparent that Saul was no longer competent to lead his people, a brilliant young military leader came forward to fill the power vacuum. His name was David. He was a man of myriad talents whom the people loved: he wrote poetry and was a musician, a skillful politician, and a military strategist. Above all, he was committed to making Israel a great nation under Yahweh.

Shortly after becoming king of Israel, David drove the Philistines from the land, earning the undying devotion of the Hebrew people. Then he moved swiftly to consolidate the tribes into a strong nation. Jerusalem became the center of worship under David, who saw to it that Baal worship was wiped out. And God made a commitment to David, a new covenant, to establish David's kingdom—and that of his heirs—forever.

David's son Solomon succeeded him on the throne, leading the nation to glorious new accomplishments. Solomon extended the national boundaries through the use of force, constructed an enormous and exquisite temple dedicated to Yahweh, and built himself a glamorous and imposing palace. Although he was known for his wisdom, Solomon lacked the spiritual character of his father. And he was all too willing to be broad-minded about combining Baal worship and Yahweh worship. Solomon pampered himself like an Oriental despot, forcing thousands of citizens into hard labor on his building projects. According to the Biblical account, written much later, Yahweh ended up denouncing Solomon and removing him from the throne.

David and Solomon inspired an exuberant nationalism that prompted one devoted author to write the great epic account of Israel's history that forms the backbone of the Hebrew Bible. This anonymous tenth-century B.C. writer is known simply as the Yahwist. His magnificent prose epic celebrates Israel's covenant faith by telling, from Abraham's day forward, the story of Israel's commitment to Yahweh. As a prologue to this history of Israel and the covenant community, the Yahwist provides a vivid account of primeval history, ranging from the story of Adam and Eve to the story of the tower of Babel. He reaches way beyond the Jewish tradition to ancient Mesopotamian myths in compiling these stories.

The guiding theme of the Yahwist's account of Hebrew history, found in the first five books of the Old Testament (the Pentateuch), is God's promise to make Israel a great and powerful nation—a nation that would be a light to all nations, the special agent for blessing humanity in Yahweh's universal plan.

None of the Yahwist's stories were new to the Israelites, but his talent for assembling them in a compelling epic framework was brilliant and revolutionary. And it was around this framework that the Hebrews would continue to build their Scriptures for centuries to come.

KEEPING THE FAITH AS THE NORTHERN KINGDOM CRUMBLES

With the death of Solomon, the kingdom of Israel quickly split into Northern and Southern sectors—with the North ruled by an old enemy of Solomon's named Jeroboam and the South ruled by Solomon's son Rehoboam. In the North, Jeroboam did his best to consolidate his kingdom by setting up new shrines for worship and inspired his people with nationalistic pride. He didn't mind making compromises with the Baal worshipers, though, and even set up some golden bulls in Yahweh's new shrines.

To his credit, Jeroboam inspired an anonymous author—known simply as the Elohist, since he refers to God as Elohim—to set down an epic history of the Israelite nation, written from the Northern Kingdom's point of view. Drawing on ancient oral traditions as did the Yahwist, the Elohist rehearses the sacred history of the chosen people from the call of Abraham and Israel through the Exodus and on to the conquest of Canaan. But, unlike the Yahwist's history, this epic exalts Moses (not David) as the supreme prophet of Israel's history, arguing for the strictest obedience to the Law and covenant that he established. In time, the two accounts became so intertwined that it's now hard to separate them as they appear in the first five books of the Bible.

The next two hundred years saw rough times for the children of Israel. There was almost constant civil war between the Northern and Southern kingdoms. Against these difficult odds, a line of great prophets poured their spiritual energies into helping the Hebrew people keep the faith—and remain true to their covenants with Yahweh.

The first of these men of God—a prophet who came to the Northern Kingdom from the desert in the early ninth century B.C.— was Elijah the Tishbite. Clad in a bizarre haircloth garment and looking out of place in the sophisticated Israelite culture, this legendary prophet denounced King Ahab for tolerating the Baal worship of his foreign wife Jezebel and building her a grandiose temple dedicated to Baal.

Elijah's was a rough-and-tumble brand of prophecy that minced no words and demanded wholesale punishments for violating Israel's covenant with God. But he showed the Hebrew people, in an unforgettable way, that Yahweh is not a nature god—not a god in the wind or the fire or the earthquake—but a wholly spiritual God who spoke to him in "a still small voice."

Following in Elijah's footsteps in the Northern Kingdom was another legendary prophet—Elisha. The account of Elisha's ministry in II Kings speaks of the prophet's remarkable spiritual feats—raising a child from the dead and healing Naaman, a Syrian general, of leprosy.

With the buildup of Assyrian power in the middle of the eighth century B.C., two more prophets emerged to chastise and comfort Israel. One was Amos, the first prophet actually to write down his insights.

The other was Hosea. Hosea perceived himself as successor to Moses and modern mediator of Israel's covenant with Yahweh. Anguished that Israel had so flagrantly broken this covenant, he forecast that God's revenge would be swift and terrible unless Israel renewed and deepened her covenant with Yahweh immediately. The doom Hosea envisioned was not long in coming. In 721 B.C., after a brutal siege of the city of Samaria, Assyria conquered Israel decisively and deported over twenty-seven thousand Hebrew people to Persia. And the Northern Kingdom was repopulated with foreigners—colonists from Syria, Babylonia, and Elam. The dream of the great Israelite nation seemed lost forever.

THE FALL OF THE SOUTHERN KINGDOM

With the fall of the Northern Kingdom of Israel, the only hope for carrying forward the covenant faith lay with the Southern Kingdom of Judah. There, in Jerusalem, the prophet Isaiah stepped forward to advise King Ahaz and console the people as they strove to ward off the Assyrian threat that had crushed Israel. Over his forty-year ministry, which began in 742 B.C., Isaiah wrote the hymns, oracles, and narratives that make up the first thirty-nine chapters of the book of Isaiah.

Sketch of Jerusalem, 1875

All that Isaiah could envision for Judah was the doom and misery that would descend upon the land on the Judgment Day of Yahweh, when God would sue His people for their breach of faith. At that time, Isaiah prophesied that the destruction of Judah would be complete except for a small remnant of righteous people who would help revive David's line of kingship, which God had covenanted to preserve forever. Isaiah promised also that a special child would be born, a Messiah who would bring salvation to the Hebrews and assure them of God's presence with them always. This would be the sign of Immanuel. When Isaiah realized that the Hebrew people didn't want to hear his message, he withdrew from society and wrote his words down in the Book of Testimony that is found between Isaiah 6:1 and 9:7.

Later, a commanding message also came from the prophet Jeremiah, whom Yahweh commissioned to sue Judah for divorce because of her infidelity to the covenant. Acting as Yahweh's attorney in the case, Jeremiah explained to the people that outward obedience to Yahweh wasn't enough. A change of heart—a "circumcision of the heart"—was needed.

Judah's new king, Josiah, was so impressed with Jeremiah's message that he threw all the Assyrian images out of the Temple in 621 B.C. As he did this, a remarkable discovery was made in the Temple—the Book of the Torah. This book turned out to be Moses' law code, which had apparently been lost for centuries. Thrilled by this find, Josiah immediately summoned his subjects to the Temple to hear the book read aloud for the very first time and to renew their commitment to the ancient covenant.

As part of the reform brought about by Josiah's discovery of the Torah, an anonymous writer, known simply as the Deuteronomic writer, composed a history of Israel and Judah from the death of Solomon in 922 B.C. to the revolution of Jehu in 842 B.C. From the point of view of the Deuteronomic writer, all of Israel's problems came from her disobedience to the Law. This material can be found in Joshua and I and II Kings. In addition, this same writer—or team of writers—summarized and celebrated the Law and teaching of Moses in the book of Deuteronomy, which was to become the foundation of Hebrew doctrine.

Not everyone was pleased, however, with Josiah's reforms or with the work of the Deuteronomic writer. The prophet Nahum, for example, said that Israel didn't deserve her punishments. It simply wasn't fair that she should be swallowed up by the Assyrians. And the prophet Habakkuk asked Yahweh how long Israel's troubles would last. He just couldn't accept the Deuteronomic writer's view of Jewish history as a matter of being rewarded or punished by God for good or bad behavior.

Initially, Jeremiah was pleased with the Deuteronomic reforms, but toward the end of his forty years as a prophet he rejected them. He felt they offered a shortsighted and nationalistic view of Israel's place in history—that they encouraged obedience to the letter of the Law while overlooking the need for deep-down regeneration.

Again, warning the Hebrew people of the need for absolute obedience to the one God, prophets like Jeremiah, Habakkuk, and Zephaniah predicted doom and destruction if their warnings weren't heeded. The destruction finally came in 587 B.C., when the Babylonian King Nebuchadnezzar invaded Jerusalem, devastated its Temple, and forced the Hebrew people to return to Babylon with him as prisoners.

Israel's only salvation, Jeremiah knew, lay in the New Covenant he had promised—a covenant of the heart. That covenant would someday be the foundation for the restoration of Jerusalem.

CHAPTER THREE

The Old Testament Marriage Covenant Lives On

THE EXILE IN BABYLON

Sometimes in a marriage there comes a moment of truth–a time when a couple face overwhelming pressures that have the potential to destroy their union. Israel confronted such pressures during its sixty-year Exile in Babylon, a period that threatened Israel's covenant with Yahweh.

Under foreign rule, the Jews fought to keep their religious traditions alive. They continued to worship Yahweh, despite the fact that they weren't in their beloved Temple in Jerusalem. And, as was usually the case throughout Jewish history, Israel's religious reformers kept the people's faith alive by insisting that they remain true to the covenant with Yahweh.

Perhaps the most unusual of these reformers was a man named Ezekiel, who served–probably as a priest–in the Temple at Jerusalem. After being taken to Babylon in the deportation of 598–597 B.C., Ezekiel beheld Yahweh seated on a throne on top of a magnificent chariot. Awed by this vision, Ezekiel agreed to deliver to the Jews Yahweh's message–a message that turned out to be one of lamentation and woe for the imminent doom of his homeland. Then, when Jerusalem finally fell in 588–587 B.C., Ezekiel's message turned to one of hope. He told the people that, even though they were like a pile of dead bones at the moment, Yahweh would put flesh on those bones and infuse them with new life.

At this same time, a historian known as the Priestly Writer prepared a revised compilation of Israel's beginnings–told from the priestly point of view. It's a richly poetic piece of prose that is now woven through the first four books of the Old Testament. The magnificent first chapter of Genesis, with its story of an orderly, seven-day creation, is an example of the Priestly Writer's majestic prose.

The greatest prophet of the Exile remains nameless. But since his work lies in chapters 40 through 55 of the book of Isaiah, modern scholars have called him Second Isaiah. In his beautiful series of poems, he gives a light-filled and joyous new interpretation of the tragic Exile experience. He announces jubilantly that Israel's deliverer is at hand. He even goes so far as to name him as Cyrus, the Persian king who was sweeping victoriously through the Fertile Crescent.

Second Isaiah's words speak to the yearning hearts of the exiles with comfort and deep love. He tells them they're like the suffering servant he portrays in his poetry. For now, they'll have to submit to affliction. But the future will bring them victory. By treading the humble path of the servant–suffering willingly for the good of humanity–Israel will usher in a glorious new age.

LIBERATION AND REBUILDING
IN JERUSALEM

As Second Isaiah predicted, Cyrus of Persia did conquer Babylon and–benevolent ruler that he was–released the entire Jewish population in the year 538 B.C. to return to Palestine. Not everyone accepted his offer, though. Some preferred to remain in Babylon, where they had lived happily enough in exile for two generations. However, many thousands did return home.

But the homecoming, which took place over a period of a hundred years or more, hardly measured up to Second Isaiah's glowing predictions. An anonymous prophet who wrote the last ten chapters of Isaiah (known usually as Third Isaiah) expresses the frustration that the Jewish people felt as they faced the stark realities of life in their demolished homeland. Their Temple was devastated. Jerusalem was in ruins. Reconstruction turned out to be slow, painful, and uninspired.

Then came the ringing rebuke of the prophets Haggai and Zechariah. They roused the people from their lethargy. Haggai told the Jews they needed to think less about personal prosperity and more about rebuilding the Temple. Inspired by these prophets, the Jews finally completed construction of a new Temple in 515 B.C. But in some ways Israel was only a shadow of her former self. Her territory was greatly reduced, her land in ruins, and her religious fervor cooled. The Israelites felt hopeless.

At this point, three prophets—Obadiah, Malachi, and Joel—cried out to the Hebrew people. Obadiah condemned Edom for seizing part of Judah's territory during the Exile. Malachi chastised the Jews for their superficial approach to worship—worship based on ritual, not love. And Joel bemoaned an infestation of locusts in Israel, saying it was surely a sign of Yahweh's anger.

Not until 445 B.C. did Israel have a leader with both the vision and the determination to rebuild Jerusalem and her crumbled walls. That man was Nehemiah, whose story is told in the books of Ezra and Nehemiah. As cupbearer in the court of the Persian king Artaxerxes, Nehemiah had achieved a position of prominence. However, when he heard how desperate and defenseless his fellow Jews in Jerusalem were, he couldn't be silent. He asked Artaxerxes to let him return to Jerusalem in order to help his fellow Israelites rebuild the crumbled walls of the city. Artaxerxes granted his request, appointing him governor of Israel. Nehemiah rushed to Jerusalem and led a valiant campaign to reconstruct the walls—a feat he accomplished in an astounding fifty-two days. He gave the people a new sense of national identity, endeavoring to whip them into strict obedience to the Torah, or Mosaic law, and telling them to stop adulterating their religion by marrying foreigners.

The south wall of the Ishtar Gate of Babylon

Not everyone, however, agreed that such severe measures were necessary. In fact, the book of Ruth, which most scholars think was written about this time, tells the touching story of how—centuries earlier—a young woman from Moab married into a Hebrew family and embraced their faith with such fervor that she remained true to it even after the death of her husband. Eventually she married a devout relative of her husband and became the great-grandmother of King David. This story clearly illustrated that foreigners could be good wives for Jewish men, no matter what Nehemiah said to the contrary!

Picking up where Nehemiah had left off in exhorting the people to obey the Torah, the priest Ezra arrived from Babylonia in about 428 B.C., leading a band of Jewish exiles back to Palestine. After that, he led the Jews in a solemn covenant renewal ceremony, in which the people vowed to obey the Law as never before–down to the last letter. More than anyone else, Ezra was responsible for reintroducing the Law to the Jerusalem community, making the people feel once again their unique love-covenant commitment to Yahweh. Ezra is usually considered the father of Judaism.

Since, thanks to the work of Ezra and Nehemiah, the primary emphasis in the postexilic community was on the Law and ritual, it's not surprising that a historian known to us as the Chronicler wrote at that time a large chunk of Hebrew history from the point of view of priestly Judaism. The Chronicler's full account can be found in I and II Chronicles, as well as in Ezra and Nehemiah.

During the postexilic period, too, priests in the new Temple collected into one hymnbook the beautiful psalms that had been written over the six preceding centuries–from about David's time forward. This glorious anthology of poetic prayers ranges from hymns of praise, to laments, to songs of thanksgiving. Tradition has it that David wrote seventy-three of the one hundred and fifty psalms in the Bible. (Actually, he wrote fewer than that; most of the psalms were written by anonymous poets over the centuries.) More than any other book in the Old Testament, Psalms celebrates the covenant community's long tradition of worshiping in the Temple–and praising God together in song.

THE WISDOM MOVEMENT AND COVENANT FAITH

Since before the time of Abraham, wise sayings and stories pondering the meaning of human life had circulated by word of mouth throughout the Fertile Crescent. They became especially popular during the postexilic period, when they were compiled for the first time. These sayings came from sages–wise men in every tribe and nation who thought deeply about how to live successfully and how to cope with human tragedy. Israel's sages were different from the rest, though. They were convinced that their wisdom was a *divine* gift, not a personal endowment. And they felt sure that no sage in history was wiser than their beloved King Solomon.

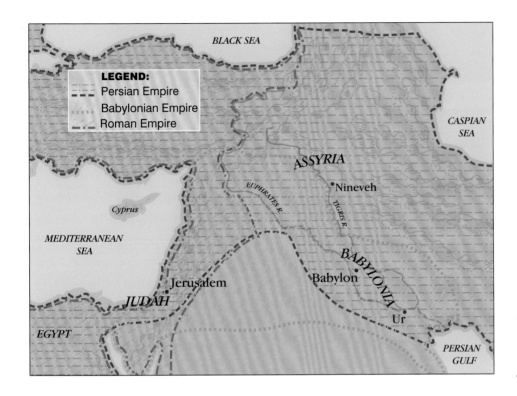

Map of three empires that overtook the Jewish people

The best-known Biblical wisdom literature is the book of Proverbs, an anthology of short statements, each summarizing simply and clearly some profound truth. According to tradition, Solomon wrote this book of the Bible, but actually it's the work of writers throughout Israel's history. And underneath all the commonsense counsel in Proverbs is a strong conviction of the postexilic Jews: that *Yahweh*, not humanity, is the source of all true wisdom.

The Bible's most dramatic piece of wisdom literature is the book of Job. According to this old legend, also recorded for the first time after the Exile, Yahweh tests Job's faithfulness by allowing Satan to rain down disaster on him. Job loses his many possessions, his children, his health. Overcome by the meaninglessness of his suffering, he denounces the God who he believes sent him these misfortunes.

At this point, however, God suddenly appears to Job in the form of a mighty whirlwind—thundering out questions that make Job understand as never before the omnipotence and glory of Yahweh. This awesome divine presence and power humbles and satisfies Job. And he feels reunited—recovenanted—with the God of his people.

Reformed and chastened by God, he rises from the ashes of his misery and rebuilds his life—blessed by Yahweh with more children and twice as many riches as before.

THE LAST YEARS BEFORE THE COMING OF JESUS CHRIST

As Judaism took firm root in the relatively peaceful atmosphere of postexilic Palestine—safe under the protective wing of the Persian Empire—the Jewish community struggled to understand how to deal with the great empire that had subdued them on the one hand and given them the freedom to return to their homeland on the other.

Some earnest Jews, like the anonymous author of the book of Esther, felt vengeful toward Persia and intolerant of any religion but their own. The author of Esther tells the story of an incredibly beautiful Jewish woman who is chosen to be queen of Persia. As queen, she discovers that an enemy of her people has persuaded the king to slaughter all the Jews in Persia. Horrified, she risks her life by begging her husband to save the Jews. He grants her request, and a bloodbath follows as the king turns his wrath on the Persians who had wanted to kill the Jews. The author's point is clear: he believes in revenge against the enemies of Yahweh's people.

The author of the book of Jonah, however, felt very differently. In what may be the most famous "fish story" of all time, he tells how Jonah—commanded by God to preach to the Assyrian capital of Nineveh—refuses to obey, on the ground that Assyria is Israel's enemy. Angry that Jonah has disobeyed Him by sailing *away* from Nineveh instead of toward it, Yahweh causes Jonah to be thrown overboard in a storm. Through a remarkable series of events, Jonah ends up being swallowed alive by an enormous fish and then vomited out of the fish's mouth onto the land. Chastened by this experience, Jonah goes to Nineveh, where he succeeds in converting the whole sinful city to belief in Yahweh. In this way he saves its large population from spiritual doom, and God strives to teach him not to be narrow-minded in his view of foreign nations.

By the fourth century B.C., a new kind of pressure was threatening to exterminate Judaism—the cultural phenomenon known as

Hellenism, the imposition of the Greek culture and language in all the lands conquered by Alexander of Macedon. Then, in 175 B.C., the king of Syria, named Antiochus IV, convinced that he was the living embodiment of the Greek god Zeus, erected an altar to himself in the middle of the Jerusalem Temple and made the worship of any god but him a capital offense.

Faced with this effort to eradicate their religion, the Jewish people waged a battle to the death to preserve their right to worship Yahweh alone and so remain true to their covenant faith. Spearheading this resistance was a band of fearless guerrillas headed by Judas Maccabeus, commonly called "the Hammer," whose zealous followers won a stunning victory over Antiochus in 165 B.C.—and thereby secured a century of religious freedom for the Jewish people.

It was during the Hammer's campaign that the book of Daniel was written. The author of Daniel, like the Maccabeans, was a member of the Hasidic sect of Jews, who believed passionately that the Jewish people should—no matter how much persecution they faced—refuse to adopt the ways of Hellenism. His message was this: the end-time is coming when all evil forces will be utterly destroyed. Therefore, to avoid doom, the Jewish people must resist Hellenism with all their hearts.

Page from an early Bible in Greek

Just how did the author of Daniel get these ideas across at a time when reading—much less *obeying*—the Torah was punishable by death? By writing in a secret code understandable only to the Jews. In the first six chapters of the book, for instance, he tells the story of Daniel and his friends—legendary Jews of the Exile period—who repeatedly disobey Babylonian law and obey the Torah, even though they face a death sentence for doing so. In each case, as in the story of Daniel in the lions' den, Yahweh delivers the Hebrew worshiper. But He also convinces the Babylonian rulers of His omnipotence—that He is in fact the only true God.

The Maccabeans' struggle to preserve Judaism and to reestablish the Jewish nation was successful, but the peace and religious freedom they won was, as mentioned earlier, short-lived. In the year 63 B.C., the forces of the Roman general Pompey imposed Roman rule in Israel. The Jews chafed under the Roman yoke and lived in hope that a member of their community of faith—the Messiah prophesied in their Scriptures—would lead them in a fight to reestablish their national identity.

For a brief time, some of them thought they had found such a leader in a young Jew named Jesus, who went about the land for three years healing sick people and preaching that the kingdom of heaven had arrived. But when the people discovered that the kingdom Jesus spoke of was a purely spiritual one—a kingdom "within" and not the triumphant Jewish nation they so desperately desired—they were deeply disappointed. Their religious leaders turned Jesus over to the Roman authorities and insisted that he be crucified.

SAVING THE HEBREW BIBLE AFTER THE DIASPORA

Finally, a generation after the crucifixion of Jesus, militant Jews rallied for one last all-or-nothing effort to throw off Roman rule. The result was crushing defeat. The Temple was destroyed, never again to be rebuilt. Most Jews left Jerusalem for other lands in what has since been called the Diaspora. Only a few stragglers remained, a mere rem-

Detail of a frieze on the Arch of Titus, Rome, depicting the devastation of Jerusalem

nant of the former populace. For the next two thousand years, the idea of an independent Jewish state was nothing more than a dream.

The only way to preserve any sense of national identity or unity in the face of these overwhelming odds was to preserve for all time the Holy Scriptures—the writings that recorded the unique love covenant between the Hebrew people and Yahweh. The Jews selected which of the many texts available should stand in the final Hebrew Biblia, or group of "little books." And they arranged these books in an order approved by their rabbis, or teachers. These books became the official Hebrew canon—the standard against which Hebrew Scripture would always be measured.

So the Hebrew Bible, known to Christians as the Old Testament, was complete so far as the Hebrew people were concerned. Their love covenant with God was sealed forever in the pages of their Scriptures. This covenant was a promise no conqueror could take away from them. Their Temple could be flattened and their people cruelly dispersed over all the earth. But their faith in God's unique promises to them remained in their hearts generation after generation. Despite all they had suffered, they still felt wedded to Yahweh and cherished their Bible as the symbol, the written record, of this union. And they awaited patiently the day when Yahweh's promises, faithfully documented in their Scriptures, would be fulfilled.

III
GROWTH
OF THE
CHRISTIAN
CHURCH
AND
SCRIPTURES

CHAPTER FOUR

The Gospels: Proclaiming the Good News

D evout Jews had been waiting for centuries. Their prophets— men like Isaiah, Zechariah, and Daniel—had promised a Messiah would come, bringing peace and the foundations of righteousness to Palestine and establishing God's kingdom all over the earth.

For some Jews this promise of a Messiah was not an urgent matter. The priestly Sadducees, for instance, were content to cooperate with their Roman conquerors. They officiated at the ceremonial rites in the Temple as they had for centuries and maintained their dominant position on the Sanhedrin, the highest religious council of the Jews. The Pharisees, on the other hand, were more impatient with Roman rule. A nonpriestly movement made up entirely of laypeople, they longed for the arrival of the Messiah.

One monastic sect, the Essenes, was so convinced the coming of the Messiah was imminent that they left Jerusalem in protest, disgusted with the secularization of Jewish thought. This sect set up a religious community at Qumran, overlooking the Dead Sea. They perceived life as a vicious battle between good and evil. Only a Messiah, they felt, could end this battle and bring about the ultimate triumph of good. Their library of Biblical and other texts, now known as the Dead Sea Scrolls, was discovered in eleven seaside caves between 1947 and 1960.

Around A.D. 30, a group of Jews in Palestine felt sure that the Messiah had actually come. They listened earnestly as the young man named Jesus called on them to repent of their sins and make room in their lives for the kingdom of God. His words were with power, healing people of all kinds of diseases—even what the Bible calls leprosy— and changing their lives so radically that they felt reborn, regenerated.

A 2,000-year-old storage jar from the caves at Qumran where, in 1947, the Dead Sea Scrolls were found by Bedouin shepherds

A few of the Jews who saw and heard Jesus acknowledged him as Christ, the Son of God. They were so sure he was the promised Messiah, and so swept up in instant love for him, that they dropped everything else in their lives and followed him. But many people refused to listen to Jesus. Even some of his followers began to desert him when they felt his uncompromising spiritual demands for reformation and regeneration.

Eventually, Jesus' message became so offensive to the Jewish authorities that they turned him over to the Romans to be put to death, as mentioned before. But even death couldn't halt his mission. Three days after he'd been buried in a stone sepulcher, Jesus reappeared to his awestruck disciples. For a number of days he met with them, telling them to carry the good news, or "gospel," of the kingdom of God and of his resurrection to the ends of the earth.

Obedient to their Master's last request, the disciples told and retold the gospel story throughout Palestine and beyond—to anyone who'd listen. And the people who believed this good news became known as Christians.

THE ORAL TRADITION

For at least twenty years after the resurrection of Jesus Christ, his life story was told by word of mouth, although it probably wasn't related as a continuous history arranged in chronological order. These oral traditions took various forms. Some are now called "pronouncement" stories—short conversations between Jesus and other people that ended with a strong pronouncement by him. Some stories centered on "miracles"—healings the Master accomplished. Then there were parables (often described as earthly stories with heavenly meanings), sayings, and similes. And in some cases the traditions were narratives about events in Jesus' life, like the accounts of his birth or his crucifixion.

As the firsthand witnesses of Jesus' career began to disappear in the middle of the first century A.D., and especially after the Romans crushed the Jewish revolt in Jerusalem in A.D. 70, some Christians became concerned that the story of Jesus might be lost altogether unless someone wrote it down. So they began recording Jesus' teachings and facts about his life. Eventually these writings were narrowed

down to four books, the Gospels—Matthew, Mark, Luke, and John.
These books became the cornerstone of the New Testament.

THE Q COLLECTION

Most scholars agree that some of the earliest written material about
Jesus was an anonymous collection now known simply as Q (short
for the German *Quelle,* meaning "source"). The Q source contained
very few narrative sections about Jesus' life. But it did document, probably from eyewitness reports, a number of Jesus' sayings, some stories
about John the Baptist, the story of the temptation of Jesus by the
devil, as well as some parables and miracles. The Q material was
almost certainly written in Aramaic, the spoken language of the Jews.

The original Q document has never been located, but scholars
feel they have found significant portions of it in the Gospels of
Matthew and Luke, particularly in the Sermon on the Mount and in
Jesus' teachings about the kingdom of heaven and the need to love
one's enemies. As a very early rendition of Jesus' teachings, Q may
well have had a special accuracy and validity.

THE GOSPEL OF MARK

The first Christian to document the events of Jesus' career in something like chronological order was the gospel writer we call Mark,
though his identity isn't certain. Writing in approximately A.D. 70,
about the time that Roman forces destroyed Jerusalem, he spoke urgently to the Jewish Christians in his community. He entreated them
to stand firm in the faith.

The Gospel of Mark was probably addressed to readers living
outside of Palestine and was intended to prove that Jesus was the
Messiah, the Son of God. So one of Mark's major themes is Jesus'
unique authority over earthly forces—demons, sin, disease, and even
the ritualized Mosaic Law. But Mark recognizes that even though the
Master can control material forces, he'll eventually have to endure
great suffering. For this reason, Mark repeatedly foreshadows the
unjust condemnation and crucifixion of Jesus.

Mark's account of Christ Jesus' ministry is filled with reassur-
ance for the Christian community. He uses urgent words like *straight-
way* and *immediately* to show how instantly available God's power was

to His beloved Son. This same power, Mark implies, is still with Christians—even in the trying times that they presently face.

Because Mark wants his readers to understand that Jesus really was Christ, he emphasizes the Master's power to quell a violent storm on the Sea of Galilee and to perform numerous miracles—miracles he describes more fully than do the other gospel writers. Further emphasizing Jesus' identity as the Son of God, Mark's Gospel recounts Jesus' transfiguration. He describes how the disciples see Jesus, his clothing radiant with spiritual light, talking with Moses and Elias. Then they hear the voice of God say, "This is my beloved Son: hear him."

In one of the key passages in Mark, Jesus predicts the destruction of the great Jerusalem Temple and a series of other catastrophic events—wars, natural disasters, and cataclysms. But after all these events, Jesus promises, the Son of man will finally come "with great power and glory" to save humanity.

In his rendition of Jesus' final supper with his disciples before his crucifixion, Mark states simply but eloquently that Jesus must give his life to save others. Mark's Gospel ends soon after with a description of the last events in Jesus' career, including his resurrection from the dead and his ascension. The rest of the story Mark has already implied—that Jesus Christ will reign forever as the Son of man prophesied in the Old Testament, and that this reign will begin *any moment now.*

THE GOSPEL OF MATTHEW

The most familiar of the four Gospels is the book of Matthew, written about A.D. 90. Although tradition has it that Jesus' disciple Matthew wrote this Gospel, the author was clearly someone who had his information secondhand, through the oral tradition, the Q source, and the Gospel of Mark. He wrote in Greek for a Greek-speaking, Christian-Jewish community, perhaps the one Paul started at Antioch. The author wanted to appeal to his community's Jewish point of view, but he was also sharply critical of Judaism and bitterly blamed the Jews for Jesus' death. For him, the *Church,* and not the Jewish nation, had become the real Israel.

Matthew's guiding purpose in writing his Gospel was to provide Jewish Christians with a manual that would instruct them on how to govern their churches and their lives. He hoped to strengthen his readers' faith in Jesus and help them understand better how to follow in his footsteps. To accomplish this, he gives the fullest account in the Bible of what has been called the Sermon on the Mount–a digest of Jesus' most important teachings. The cornerstone of this sermon is a series of short declarations, or "sayings," now called the Beatitudes. These sayings proclaim the blessings that sincere Christians will receive as they humbly live their faith. The sermon, as Matthew gives it, requires much more than surface and legalistic conformity to God's requirements. It demands a change of *heart*–more love, forgiveness, and purity.

A fragment of a handwritten Greek Bible from the sixth century A.D. (Mark 7)

As Matthew saw it, Jesus' whole career was the unfoldment of God's plan–a plan previewed in Old Testament prophecy. So, time and again, he quotes the Septuagint (the Greek translation of the Hebrew Bible) to show how Jesus' mission has fulfilled Scripture.

Matthew's history of Jesus' lifework is tightly organized. He opens with a genealogy that traces Jesus' lineage back to Abraham– demonstrating the Master's direct descent from the father of the Jewish people. The Gospel divides into five parts. Each part begins by relating events in Jesus' career and ends with a discussion of those events. Matthew closes the Gospel with an account of the crucifixion and resurrection.

The Gospel of Matthew is full of advice for church members. At first Matthew tells them that their key mission is to the Jews, the lost sheep of the house of Israel. But, at the end of the book, he shows how the risen Christ has opened up the Church's mission to the whole world, to both Jew and Gentile. Matthew is the only gospel writer to comment on the founding of the Church in connection with Peter's acknowledgment that Jesus was the Christ. Matthew counsels Christians to be patient–with each other and with their lot as outcasts from Jerusalem. They need to be faithful and watchful, trusting that at the Day of Judgment the weeds (tares) among their members will be purged and the pure wheat, the faithful members, will be saved. In the meantime, they must expect that at any moment the Son of man will come again to save the world. And they can thank God that the Christ is already present in their *hearts*.

THE GOSPEL OF LUKE

Luke was a cultured and literary Christian, apparently a Gentile. He wrote his account of Jesus' life sometime between A.D. 70 and 90. Like all public figures of the day, he spoke Greek. And, like Matthew, he based his record on Mark's Gospel and followed its general sequence of events. But he writes for a much broader audience and has a far more expansive view of the Church as a universal, rather than a Jewish, institution.

Luke's main purpose is to show how crucially important the Church is to humanity—even though, according to Luke, the Day of Judgment is just around the corner. The Church is urgently needed, he argues, to help usher in the New Age of Christ and to ensure that God's plan in history will be carried out.

The Gospel of Luke is actually the first half of a two-part volume by the same author. It's made up of both the Gospel and the book of Acts (a history of how the followers of Jesus established the early Christian Church).

Above all, Luke wants his readers to feel new faith in Christ. So his two-part book could be thought of as one long sermon designed to win his readers' hearts, to convince them that the Christ has come. And he includes a good deal of material that's not found in the other Gospels—for instance, the parables of the good Samaritan, the prodigal son, Lazarus and the rich man, and the publican and the Pharisee.

The main body of Luke's account divides into three chrono-logical sections that some scholars have called "epochs." The first of these periods, extending from ancient Israel through John the Baptist, brings out how the Spirit operated in the births of John the Baptist and Jesus. The second, covering the ministry of Jesus, shows the spirit of God working in the Master's life and continuing in the mission of the Church. The third period, which begins with Jesus' ascension, covers the momentous events following the Day of Pentecost, which Luke recounts at the beginning of the book of Acts.

A key theme running through this whole Gospel is that Christians simply can't limit their mission to the Jews. Christ's kingdom must embrace *universal* humanity. With this in mind, Luke traces Jesus' lineage clear back to Adam (the father of the whole human race) rather than just to Abraham (the father of the Jewish nation).

True, the Christian ministry must start at Jerusalem, the spiritual capital of the Jewish faith. But from Jerusalem, where the disciples receive the Holy Ghost, the voice of the Church must ultimately reach out *to the world*—as indeed it does in the book of Acts.

THE GOSPEL OF JOHN

For years, the early Church maintained that Jesus' disciple John wrote this Gospel. But some scholars now say that the book was written between A.D. 90 and 100, too late to have been a firsthand account of the Master's lifework. They believe it was written by a Jewish convert to Christianity, perhaps someone raised in a synagogue some distance from Jerusalem. Whether he was the Apostle John or not, the author of the book of John was a profoundly spiritual Christian.

In some ways the book of John is similar to Matthew, Mark, and Luke (which are often called the "Synoptic" Gospels because they have so much in common). But in other ways the Gospel of John is worlds apart from the Synoptics. John rearranges the chronologies found in the Synoptics and reinterprets the events in Jesus' life. Also, he places Jesus' ministry largely in Jerusalem rather than in Galilee, leaves out all of Jesus' parables, and includes sayings not found in

Artist's rendering of Jesus with his disciples, from The Book of Common Prayer, Church of England, 1660

Matthew, Mark, and Luke. He introduces lengthy discourses on subjects treated only lightly in the other Gospels–subjects like truth, eternal life, light versus darkness, blindness versus sight, and glory. Often he speaks in symbols with more than one level of meaning. And he records a number of astounding assertions Jesus made about himself.

One of John's major purposes in writing his book was to help the Jewish Christians deal with their disappointment that, in their view, Christ still hadn't come. He meets this concern by arguing that the Christ is already present in their hearts, bringing them eternal life now and in time to come. To support this argument, John gives his readers a new theological insight into Jesus' life, death, and resurrection. His message is essentially this: Jesus is the only Son of God, acting on God's behalf to redeem the world from sin.

Structurally, the Gospel divides into two parts. The first of these–chapters 1 through 12–tells the story of Jesus' ministry. This part includes seven miracle stories, or "signs," interwoven with discussions explaining the significance of each miracle. The first sign, which appears only in John's Gospel, describes a wedding feast where Jesus turns water into wine. Symbolically, on one level, the wine represents the new and vibrant life that Christianity pours into Judaism's traditional way of thinking. In a sense, all the signs show how Christ constantly infuses new life into the Christian community. And, in that

Jesus with his disciples at the "Last Supper," from The Book of Common Prayer, Church of England, 1660

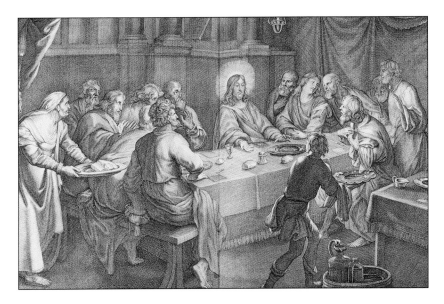

sense, they all point toward the death and resurrection of Jesus, which John describes in the final chapters of his Gospel as the climactic hour when Jesus fulfills the promise of the signs.

The second part of John's Gospel begins with the "Last Supper," which has special significance for John. The poignant picture of Jesus tenderly washing his disciples' feet following the meal appears only in John and sets an example for Christian discipleship. And John explains in his account of the Last Supper what Church truly is—a community endowed by Christ with the Holy Spirit. It's the way God shows His love for humanity. And Jesus' life is the supreme model the Church will always follow.

THE FOUR GOSPELS

Four perspectives on Jesus' lifework—that's what Matthew, Mark, Luke, and John give us. No single gospel account is definitive or complete. Each one is colored by the author's background and understanding of Jesus Christ. If we read Matthew alone, we see Jesus primarily as the Jewish Messiah. If we read John alone, we lose some of the historical Jesus but gain an understanding of the eternal Christ.

Considered as a whole, the four Gospels add up to a collective witness that's both fair-minded and convincing, both theologically balanced and historically credible. The Gospels represent numerous oral and written perspectives on the Master—all merging into one dazzling kaleidoscopic view.

It's up to each reader to measure these four views of the Master against one another, sift them together, and let the real Jesus Christ emerge.

CHAPTER FIVE

Christianity Takes Root in the Roman World

THE DAY OF PENTECOST

The Master's words had been very clear just before he ascended. His disciples were to tell the story of his life and teaching, of his crucifixion and resurrection, *everywhere*—in Jerusalem, in all Judea, in the neighboring territories, "in all the world."

So, immediately after he passed from their sight, the disciples began to preach the risen Christ in Jerusalem. Then, shortly after the ascension, came the Day of Pentecost, the traditional harvest festival of the Jews. A sound like "a rushing mighty wind" filled the house where the faithful band of Jesus' followers were worshiping. As the book of Acts describes it, "tongues like as of fire" hovered over the congregation—and everyone present received the Holy Spirit. With this divine inspiration, they began to speak in a multitude of languages.

Jews who had gathered in Jerusalem from all over the empire—as far away as Mesopotamia, Egypt, and Rome—discovered to their amazement that they could actually understand what Jesus' followers were saying. "We do hear them speak in our tongues the wonderful works of God," they said.

Jesus' disciple Peter explained to the huge crowd that they were witnessing the fulfillment of Scripture. The prophet Joel had predicted that this would occur—that God would, in the last days, "pour out" His Spirit so that ordinary people would be able to speak of God and to prophesy.

With this new impetus from the Holy Spirit, the apostles—especially Peter, James, and John—went on to tell and retell the story of their Master's lifework. As they did, their accounts probably became increasingly rich and distinct. It's likely, for instance, that they filled in

45

details they'd left out in those first breathless days after the resurrection and that they melded together the various accounts they'd heard about Jesus in order to emphasize the significance of his ministry.

As the Jerusalem Christians contemplated the various descriptions they heard of Jesus' teachings, they reread the Hebrew Scriptures in the light of what they'd heard and seen of Jesus' life. And in that way it became stunningly clear to many of them that Jesus' words and works, his trials and final triumph, all fulfilled Biblical prophecy. This conviction lit up the Old Testament with brilliant new meaning. And this new meaning, in turn, became part of the evolving gospel story, a story that was winning converts by the thousands.

The high priest in the Temple resented—and feared—the apostles' popularity, though, and saw to it that they were put in prison. But God delivered them during the night and gave them the strength to continue speaking boldly.

As the infant Church grew and prospered, however, it met more persecution—especially from a young rabbinical student named Saul, who did all he could to exterminate followers of "the Way" and their gospel message. Convinced that the new "Jesus" sect might pollute—or even supplant—the pure Jewish faith, he allowed Stephen, a zealous leader of the Jerusalem church, to be stoned to death. And he dragged countless other sincere members of the Church off to prison. Many then fled from the city.

The apostles being freed from prison by an angel, from an 1824 English Bible

Yet this persecution only served to spread Jesus' message beyond Jerusalem. Peter preached the Word widely, perhaps in Antioch and in the cities and countryside of Asia Minor. And Philip ventured into Samaria and Gaza with news of the risen Christ.

So it was, in the days and months after the ascension, that a "new testament" developed—a body of writing that told the story of Jesus' followers and their church. This New Testament began as an oral tradition, one that solidified and refined itself almost daily as the gospel preaching fanned out to a wider audience.

THE APOSTLE PAUL

Then, a few years after Jesus' ascension, Saul was converted to
Christianity and took on the new name Paul. While traveling to the
city of Damascus with the intent of further persecuting Christians, he
was suddenly enveloped in heavenly light, and Jesus was revealed
to him. Temporarily, this experience blinded Saul, until a Christian
named Ananias healed him and preached the gospel to him in
Damascus. Immediately, Saul's whole nature was transformed, and
he wanted more than anything to share his new love for Christ.

From this starting point about A.D. 35, Paul preached his revelation with an intensity and dedication that never waned—in Arabia,
Syria, Asia Minor, Achaea, Macedonia, and eventually Rome, where
he was executed about A.D. 62.

Throughout his career, Paul met stiff resistance from the Jews,
from government authorities, and from those who worshiped pagan
gods. He was imprisoned and narrowly escaped death several times
on his long missionary journeys throughout the Aegean and Mediterranean region. And he faced opposition from *within* the Christian
community, particularly when he had to convince the apostles in
Jerusalem that the Gentile Christians did not need to submit to
Jewish practices.

*A marble road in Ephesus,
one of many roads that
aided Paul in his journeys
to spread his message of
Christianity throughout
the world*

Wherever Paul found a response to his preaching, he strove to unify Christians within a very simple church organization. At times, he was able to stay a year or more in a single location–preaching, healing, and encouraging his brothers and sisters in Christ. When he moved on, he stayed in touch with the churches he'd visited by sending fellow workers such as Timothy or Titus to them and by writing these churches long letters, or "epistles."

Paul's first known epistle was probably written during his second missionary journey through Asia Minor and Greece. Most of his letters were written to specific churches. Almost always, these letters emphasize that the crucifixion and resurrection of Jesus provide certain proof that he was Christ. These letters also stress the need for unity and love among Christians, urging them to be patient with persecution and with each other.

I AND II THESSALONIANS

Among the earliest letters Paul wrote were two that went to the church he, along with his assistant Timothy, had founded at Thessalonica, which was situated on a major trade route in Greece. The first of these epistles, now known as I Thessalonians, may have been written from Corinth in A.D. 50 to 52, just a short while after Paul left Thessalonica. In this letter, he tells the largely Gentile congregation that he's pleased to have learned from Timothy's recent visit that the church has stood firm, despite persecution. What they need to do now, he explains tenderly, is *maintain* their new life in Christ in all ways and be faithful in marriage and evenhanded in their dealings with others, as they await "the day of the Lord."

Shortly after Paul sent his first letter to the Thessalonians, he wrote them another letter. This second epistle emphasizes the same points as the first but has a more businesslike tone. It's primarily concerned with straightening out a controversy that has stirred up the church members. Apparently some of the local Christians feel that Christ's kingdom has already arrived and that somehow they've missed out on it. But such is not the case, Paul reassures them. Christ's kingdom has yet to come. And when it does come, every faithful Christian will be part of it.

GALATIANS

A few years after I and II Thessalonians were written, Paul wrote a letter that was circulated and read by the churches in the province of Galatia, an area of Asia Minor. Despite suffering from chronic illness, he had established these churches, possibly during his first missionary journey.

Paul opens his letter with a feisty defense of his claim to be a fully endowed apostle—one who was specially appointed to preach the gospel to the Gentiles. Then he notes that now the church members, whom he calls "foolish," have allowed some people to confuse them about circumcision, claiming that this rite is as necessary to Christians as it is to Jews. Paul says this is false doctrine.

He tells the Galatians that they need to be "crucified in Christ," as he has been. They need to make Christianity their own, and let the Spirit create in them a new life charged with joy and love. And they need to walk in the Christ Truth that makes men and women equal, side-by-side co-workers in both marriage and church. The gospel of Christ is freely available to all humanity, Paul says, and God's saving grace depends on *faith in Christ,* not *works of the Law.* Legalism and ritualism must not be mixed up with Christianity—which frees men and women from mere ritualistic requirements of the Law.

I AND II CORINTHIANS

In his two letters to the Christian community at Corinth, Paul again reaffirms his authority as an apostle "through the will of God." And not only that. He explains that he has also *suffered* for Christ—dedicating his very life to spreading the gospel and healing the sick.

The two books of Corinthians represent three, or possibly four, letters in an ongoing correspondence between Paul and the Corinthians. The city of Corinth was a cosmopolitan city, known for its immorality. It was made up of Greeks, Romans, Jews, and other people from the Middle East. So it's understandable that the small church Paul helped set up in A.D. 51 and 52 had difficulty coping with the many pagan cultures there.

The Corinthian church began like most of the churches Paul founded—as a "house-church" where converts lived, worshiped, and

The Temple of Apollo in Corinth

worked at some trade like leather making. In his letters, therefore, Paul offers the Corinthians counsel on living and worshiping together harmoniously. And in answer to a number of questions they'd sent him, he gives them advice on moral and social matters like marriage, sexual behavior, and finances. Paul tells the church members to beware of preachers like Apollos, who apparently has captivated the local congregations with his eloquence. He tells them that only God's *grace* will attract people to their church. And members of the church should be unified, realizing that dissension within the church body violates the body of Christ. True, all members serve the church in different capacities—as apostles, prophets, teachers, healers, administrators. But these offices must work *together* in love. Then, in the thirteenth chapter of I Corinthians, Paul makes a dynamic statement about the power of spiritual love, saying it's a virtue that surpasses all others. It transforms those who give *and* receive it by the power of the Holy Spirit.

Paul tells the Corinthians that they have to make a choice: to follow either Adam's path of sin and death or the path of salvation and immortality taken by Jesus Christ. In raising Jesus from the dead, Paul explains, God has given humanity proof of His love and the promise of good things to come. The end of the age will bring the fulfillment of those good things—total transformation for humankind.

Many scholars think that Paul wrote II Corinthians in A.D. 55 or 56, perhaps a year or more after he wrote I Corinthians. They believe this second letter is a composite of several letters that he wrote to the church as it struggled to keep the faith and to solve a number of internal problems. Paul's main purpose in II Corinthians is to help the church members keep their thoughts and actions in line with Christ. He pleads with them, chastises them, and inspires them to reform—even though he's quite aware that they sometimes chafe under his correction. "The more abundantly I love you," he writes, "the less I be loved."

Paul stresses that Christian salvation requires a person to be "absent from the body and present with the Lord." And he reminds the Corinthians of the ancient Jewish covenant with God by describing Christ's relationship with the Church as a love-filled marriage. The Christians in Corinth should stay true to this marriage, he says, and not "be corrupted from the simplicity that is in Christ."

ROMANS

Paul's letter to the church in Rome, written between A.D. 56 and 58, is his longest epistle. It was also one of his last. The later letters ascribed to him may have been written by his followers. Because this letter calmly reviews Paul's basic theological themes, it stands as one of his most influential statements. The Roman church was the only one of the churches Paul wrote to that he himself hadn't founded. It had apparently been established some years before and had evolved from a Jewish-Christian group to a predominantly Gentile congregation.

In this letter, which Paul wrote while visiting Corinth again, he introduces himself to the Roman congregation and lets them know in no uncertain terms that he's planning to visit them soon. His work in Asia Minor and Greece is complete, he explains, and he makes a strong appeal for the Romans' support as he moves forward with hopes of evangelizing the western Mediterranean as far as Spain. His tone is warm, though he affirms his authority to address them as the divinely appointed Apostle to the Gentiles.

In Romans, Paul reviews his position on some major theological issues. He points out, for instance, that Jesus' mission fulfills Biblical prophecy. But he also argues that Christians are under no obligation to obey the ritual requirements of the Torah. What is required, he says, is a circumcision—a cleansing—"of the heart." Through this cleansing a person establishes a right relationship with God and wipes away his or her sin. "The law of the Spirit of life in Christ Jesus hath made me free from the law of sin and death," he writes.

To Paul, Jesus' crucifixion and resurrection have the power to regenerate humanity. It was Adam's disobedience that brought sin and death. But it's Christ Jesus' *obedience* that has reunited men and women with their creator and given them freedom and eternal life. What a person has to do to receive God's grace, Paul says, is remain faithful like Abraham did and believe totally in God's promises. Therefore, the members of the Christian community in Rome must let their faith and love burn brightly. They must trust that God is in control of their destiny and that His purpose will bring the triumph of good.

LETTERS FROM PRISON

Paul did finally arrive in Rome. He was sent there, however, as a prisoner, as described in Acts, chapters 22 through 28. Most scholars believe that he never went to Spain but was executed in Rome between A.D. 62 and 65. As a Roman citizen, Paul may have been allowed to choose where he lived, though he was under house arrest, confined with his Roman guard. But he continued to receive members of the Christian community and to preach and teach the gospel.

In Rome, Paul wrote at least three other letters: two addressed to churches and one to an individual. One of the letters went to Philippi, the first church he'd founded in Europe. Paul had a special affection for the members of this church. In fact, the letter he wrote

Fourteenth-century mosaic of St. Paul from Kariye Camii, an early Christian church in Istanbul

them, called Philippians, may have been his last. In it, he assures his friends at Philippi that all is well with him, even though he's in prison and may be condemned to death. Yet they should rejoice with him, knowing that his tribulations can only advance the cause of Christianity.

The second of these letters, addressed to the church at Colossae, was written either by Paul or by one of his followers—possibly after his death. The author is concerned about heresy in the church there. Scholars aren't certain exactly what the nature of the heresy was—human philosophy perhaps, or Jewish legalism, or angel worship. But the writer's overriding message is that the Colossians should abandon this heresy and measure up to their Christian ideals.

Paul's third prison letter is addressed to a friend in Colossae named Philemon. Apparently, Onesimus, Philemon's slave, had run away after possibly robbing his master. In Rome, Onesimus met Paul and was converted to Christianity. He was then a great help to Paul, and the two became close friends. So Paul urges Philemon to accept Onesimus back and to consider him a full-fledged, reformed brother in Christ rather than to inflict the severe punishment that normally would have been due a runaway slave.

THE APOSTOLIC HERITAGE

By around A.D. 65, both Peter and Paul had laid down their lives for Christianity. By the end of the century, most of the apostles were gone.

But they left behind a well-established Church—one that had spread with amazing speed to the farthest reaches of the Roman Empire, one that persecution couldn't destroy.

At the time Jesus ascended, his followers were barely known. But the apostles—and especially Paul—changed that perception forever. They made sure, with every sermon they preached and with every letter they wrote, that people understood one thing: they spoke in "the name of Jesus Christ of Nazareth." They let everyone know that the good news they preached was distinctive. True, it fulfilled the promises of the Hebrew Bible. Jesus *was* the Messiah the Jews had expected. But the apostles left no doubt that Jesus made a *new* covenant. And so his followers needed to found a *Church* to preserve, propagate, and record for all time the revolutionary truths that he had taught.

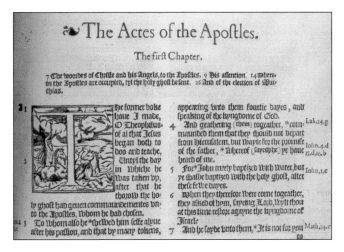

Title page from the second folio version of the Bishops' Bible, 1572

It was the Apostle Paul who, above all others, took on the awesome responsibility of establishing that Church. Without his passionate commitment and dogged zeal, Christianity might never have spread much beyond Palestine. Without his tender and sometimes tough stewardship, the churches he founded all over the Roman Empire might have become infected with heresy or faded out altogether. Without the Apostle Paul, primitive Christianity might never have taken root in the Roman world.

CHAPTER SIX

The Early Church Moves Forward

In a burst of nationalism, Jews in Palestine revolted against Roman oppression in A.D. 66. The emperor's son, Titus, retaliated by ruthlessly crushing the revolt, sacking Jerusalem, and demolishing the Jewish Temple in A.D. 70. The remaining Jews were brutally dispersed from their homeland.

The Christian community fled Jerusalem and ultimately carried the teachings of Christ Jesus to the far ends of the Roman Empire. Jerusalem was no longer the center of Christianity. So Christians, banished from their homeland, could only live in anticipation of the kingdom of God—when those who had persecuted them would be punished and those who believed in Jesus would be justified.

But when the kingdom of God hadn't come by the end of the first century, Christians were hard-pressed to explain *why* and were forced to redefine the purpose of their Church. Beyond that, they faced a leadership crisis with the deaths of the major apostles—including Peter, James, and Paul. So a new generation of Christians emerged to lead the Church forward.

A Roman soldier from a frieze in Ephesus

These second- and third-generation Christians began to write down the essential teachings of Christianity. One of their guiding purposes in doing this was to strengthen and unify the fledgling Church. To this end, they stood firmly in the tradition of the beloved apostles. But they also worked within the apostolic tradition to meet *new* challenges the Church faced as Christianity continued to take hold in the Roman world.

SPEAKING WITH APOSTOLIC AUTHORITY

Early Christian tradition had it that the Gospels of Matthew and John were written by Jesus' disciples. Many people thought that the author of Mark was John Mark, who accompanied Paul on at least one of his

Steps up to Mars' Hill in Athens, where Paul preached (Acts 17:22–31)

missionary journeys. The author of Luke was thought to have been the friend and companion of Paul. But many scholars now believe that these Gospels were written under assumed names.

Most of the other New Testament writings were also attributed to disciples–like John, James, Peter, and Jude. This was done to honor the disciples and to perpetuate their teachings.

It was natural for these later New Testament writers to follow the usual letter format of the day–a format so successfully used by Paul. They began their letters with greetings and ended them with blessings, as Paul had done. This type of "apostolic letter" was a way of speaking with and instructing the Christian field–a way that had worked well in the past. But whereas Paul's letters had been newsy and filled with advice for specific churches, the later letters were often more like sermons.

ACTS

The book of Acts is part two of a two-volume work known as Luke-Acts. This fast-moving narrative of the first thirty-five years of the Christian Church begins where the Gospel of Luke leaves off–with the ascension of Jesus. It ends with Paul's imprisonment in Rome. Acts divides into two sections. Chapters 1 through 12 focus largely on the missionary work of Peter in and around Jerusalem. Chapters 13 through 28 document Paul's missionary work in Asia Minor, Greece, and Rome.

Acts records the dramatic story of Christianity's expansion from a small Jewish sect into a much larger movement that would eventually have worldwide influence. Its theme song is this: Christianity must move, as Peter and Paul did, beyond the confines of

Judaism into the spiritually starving Gentile world. The author wanted above all to help Christians know something of the glory and success of their faith and to feel the power of the Holy Ghost working with them.

EPHESIANS

The early Church thought that Paul was the author of Ephesians. But many present-day scholars believe the book was written between A.D. 80 and 90 by a close friend of the apostle. They think he wrote the letter to be circulated to the churches in Asia Minor rather than just to Christians at Ephesus.

These churches were under heavy stress—persecuted by the Romans from without and suffering from lack of commitment from within. So the writer strives to give the churches new heart by reminding them of God's infinite power, His abounding grace, the need for unity in the Church, and the equality of Gentile and Jew in God's eyes.

More than all else, Ephesians emphasizes that peace and love must be the primary qualities of the Christian community. And in order to survive in this age, the writer says, Christians need to "put on the whole armour of God" and "be strong in the Lord, and in the power of his might."

Illustration of Peter being delivered from prison (Acts 12), from an 1824 English Bible

HEBREWS

Written sometime between A.D. 90 and 95, the book of Hebrews is not so much a letter as a sermon. It's addressed to Jewish Christians who need to understand how the Old Testament tradition fits in with the coming of the Christ. Using over a hundred passages from the Hebrew Bible to prove his point, the author argues that Jesus Christ is the new high priest and that his way of worship supersedes the traditional Jewish priestly system. Yet the author feels the Hebrew covenant tradition is still alive and valid. It needs simply to be rethought in terms of Christ's new status as the eternal Son of God—a high priest superior to the Old Testament priesthood.

*Theatre at Ephesus, where
Paul preached to multitudes*

So how should believers respond to Christ? They should culti-
vate the kind of faith Jesus himself perfected. The present age, the
author explains, will come to an end, and Christ will come a "second"
time. But until this happens, Christians should follow the examples
set by the Old Testament men and women, who obeyed God's commands without doubting. In other words, Christians in this age should
live upright lives and "let brotherly love continue."

REVELATION

Tradition has it that St. John wrote the book of Revelation in a small,
dark cave on the Isle of Patmos, where he'd been exiled. The book
features apocalyptic visions like those in the Old Testament book of
Daniel, but the author also speaks as a prophet. This magnificent
visionary book was written at a time of severe persecution—perhaps
about A.D. 96, when the Emperor Domitian was imprisoning and
executing Christians all over his realm.

Telling his readers that his message comes directly from Jesus, John says that Christians must endure persecution, even martyrdom, with the greatest faith, knowing that Christ will soon come to save them. Those who stand firm in their beliefs will witness the ultimate triumph of good over evil. And they'll see the New Jerusalem descend from heaven and transform the world.

John's revelation contains seven visions, each made of seven parts. The first vision includes seven letters to the churches in Asia Minor. Running through all these letters is this basic message: the churches need to live their faith better—no matter what trials they have to face. And, Jesus says in the vision, "To him that overcometh will I grant to sit with me in my throne, even as I also overcame, and am set down with my Father in his throne." After these letters, John describes six visions of the warfare between Christ and the forces of Satan, or evil, who represents all those who are working against God and His believers. The Revelator pictures Satan's hosts in vivid, symbolic images—a huge flesh-eating dragon and a seven-headed beast with ten horns, a leopard's body, a lion's mouth, and a bear's feet.

For a time, John says, it may seem as if the forces of evil are winning the heroic struggle. But Christians shouldn't despair. Christ will eventually wipe out the power of evil. Throughout his visions, John portrays the glory of God, culminating in his vision of a new

Patmos, a Greek island in the Aegean Sea, where John spent several years in exile

heaven and a new earth—and the establishment of the New Jerusalem. In this New Jerusalem, he explains, there will be no temple, "for the Lord God Almighty and the Lamb are the temple of it."

JAMES

Although the book of James begins with a letter-style salutation, it's actually a treatise like the book of Hebrews. Some scholars think the writer was Jesus' brother James, but the author may have been a later "teacher."

Using a question-and-answer format, James contrasts faith and works—the works of the Law. For him, "perfect law" is at the heart of true Christian worship. But this law isn't the Mosaic code. It's the "law of liberty," requiring Christians to be "doers of the word, and not hearers only." This law requires Christians to curb the tongue, stifle the passions, forsake luxury, keep free from disputes, and care for widows and orphans.

Using the examples of Abraham and Rahab, James explains that "faith without works is dead." He urges the followers of Christ to wait with patience for the day of the Lord, taking Job as their example. Finally, he reminds them of the power of prayer to heal the sick and sinning. "The effectual fervent prayer of a righteous man availeth much," he tells them.

I PETER

The author of I Peter probably wrote his epistle sometime during the last decade of the first century A.D. He urges the persecuted churches in Asia Minor to think of their trials as a purification, preparing them for "the appearing of Jesus Christ." He tells them they are "lively stones," building blocks in the community of faith. They must be long-suffering in the face of persecution, respectful toward authority, and united in spirit. His message rings with certainty that Christ *will come* and that the faithful will be glorified.

I, II, AND III JOHN

These books address a spiritual crisis within the Christian community. In the first epistle of John is a general letter to the churches. It tells them they're in danger of losing their faith. And it warns against a breakdown in morals and dissension within the Church. These subjects intersect, I John explains, because the key ingredient of Christianity is love. God *is* Love, the epistle says, and Christians are under the new commandment to love one another. And, in a message highlighted by vivid contrasts between good and evil, light and darkness, John exhorts his readers to "walk in the light."

The second epistle of John, probably written a few years after I John, is a letter addressed to "the elect lady and her children"—that is, to the Church and her members. In it, the author urges Christians to love one another and to reject heresies denying that Christ Jesus has "come in the flesh."

The third epistle of John, addressed to a Christian named Gaius, continues along the same line. The author is especially concerned that a man named Diotrephes has refused to extend hospitality to some of John's disciples. This letter explains that Gaius should do "that which is good," because, as the letter says, "he that doeth good is of God."

THE PASTORAL EPISTLES

The author of the Pastoral epistles—I and II Timothy and Titus—urges Christians to hold fast to their faith until Christ's kingdom comes. These letters are called "pastoral" because they show such a pastorlike or shepherding concern and love for the spiritual welfare of the congregations they address.

The writer honors Paul by portraying him as the author of these letters and his travel companions, Timothy and Titus, as the recipients. But many scholars think the letters were written much later—in the first quarter of the second century A.D.

These three books address concerns that were common to many of the churches at this time: the needs to keep Christian doctrine pure, to avoid the allurements of "uncertain riches," and to care for widows and their families. These pastoral letters provide counsel for churches that are now made up of largely Gentile congregations—churches that still have no authoritative collection of Scripture, no creed, and, in many cases, no defined moral tradition. The author is very direct in addressing the need for sound doctrine and morals.

He also warns his readers against false doctrines like Gnosticism, emperor worship, and astrology. And he teaches a strict code of moral conduct for all leaders in the Church, since they need to be examples for the believers. They must live absolutely pure lives, undefiled by immorality and debauchery. The author explains that right moral values are part of sound doctrine, and both are needed as Christians await the appearing of Christ. Above all, he says, church members need to hold faithfully to the apostolic teaching, avoiding both heresy and rigid conservatism.

JUDE

Like the Pastoral epistles, the little book of Jude was probably written sometime between A.D. 110 and 130. It's a stern warning to Christians to be wary of "ungodly men" who pervert the gospel of truth and defy authority. Such people are sinners, the author says, and will have to reckon with divine justice. Speaking with the voice of the Apostle Peter, the author is, like Jude, concerned that Christians should keep the teachings of Christ pure. This they can do only by living their religion and taking it beyond faith to "knowledge"—to the practical application of Christian truths.

Paul and Barnabas probably came up the Kestros River to this bridge in Perga

II PETER

The last book of the New Testament to be written down was II Peter, which many scholars date between A.D. 130 and 150. Writing in the name of the Apostle Peter, the author is, like Jude, concerned that church members should hold to traditional Christian beliefs. Those who teach something other than traditional Christian doctrine, he says, will lead their followers into licentiousness and slavery to sin. True Christian teachers, on the other hand, lead their followers to salvation.

The second coming of Christ is certain, the author says. So Christians should strive to "grow in grace, and in the knowledge of our Lord and Saviour Jesus Christ." Then they will realize "new heavens and a new earth, wherein dwelleth righteousness."

IV
DRAWING
THE LINE
BETWEEN
CANON AND
APOCRYPHA

CHAPTER SEVEN

The Old and New Testament Canons

It would have been natural for early Christians to ask themselves questions about their faith, especially after the Master and the apostles were no longer with them. Questions like: Who was this man Jesus, and what did he teach? What does it really mean to be a Christian? What do we Christians believe in, and how should we act? What kind of organization should a church have?

Most Christians felt these questions could best be answered by establishing a body of sacred writings, or Scripture, that would preserve the teachings of Jesus and the apostles accurately and clearly. So, in the first and second centuries A.D., numerous Christians recorded their understanding of these teachings, as we've noted in previous chapters. They did this in much the same way as our modern newspapers and electronic media cover an important political or religious event—from a variety of standpoints. And just as some of today's news media cover a story more reliably than others, some early Christian writers reported on the history of Jesus and his followers more responsibly than others.

By the middle of the second century A.D., a torrent of Christian literature had flooded the Roman world. Some of it measured up to the highest standards of the Christian community, but some was closer to fiction than fact. So, slowly but inevitably, Christians had to examine each piece of holy writing to determine whether it represented their faith fairly. The literature that did measure up became known as *canon,* a Greek word meaning "a rule or standard," or "a measuring rod." The literature that came up short fell into disuse. Questionable literature became known as "apocryphal," that is, of doubtful value and authenticity. In time, the canonical Christian writings became known as the "New Testament" or "New Covenant"—the Christian counterpart to the "Old Covenant" of the Hebrew Bible.

THE HEBREW CANON

It's important to understand that the New Testament canon was built on the foundations of the Hebrew canon, which was finalized in the first century A.D. After the Romans sacked Jerusalem in A.D. 70, they drove the Jews to the far ends of the empire. Desperate to preserve their religious teachings and traditions in the face of this calamity, the Jews moved quickly to put their Scriptures in final form.

The Hebrew people and their prophets had repeatedly, through the years, affirmed the absolute authority of the "Torah" (Genesis through Deuteronomy) as the basis for their religious and civil Law. Probably the first time the book of the Torah was formally canonized was in the seventh century B.C., as we've said earlier. The Torah had been discovered by workers who were rebuilding the Temple. Israel's King Josiah immediately ordered that the book of Deuteronomy be read aloud to the Hebrew people, who were so awed by its message that they joined with the king in a Passover celebration that amounted to a national canonization ceremony.

Another part of the Hebrew canon that was accepted by most Jews was the body of writings called the "Prophets." Though they didn't carry quite the authority of the Torah, these writings had been dear to the hearts of Jews for centuries. They include the historical books of Joshua, Judges, I and II Samuel, and I and II Kings, as well as the great prophetic writings of Isaiah, Jeremiah, Ezekiel, and the Twelve "Minor" prophets (Hosea through Malachi).

A third section of the Hebrew canon, the "Writings," was more open to question than the Torah or the Prophets, although Jewish rabbis eventually decided in favor of placing them in the canon. These books include Ruth, Esther, Job, Psalms, Proverbs, Ecclesiastes, and Song of Solomon.

What writings did the Jews leave *out* of their Bible? A number of Apocryphal or questionable books in both Greek and Hebrew that had been circulating in the Jewish community. Foremost among these books were the Apocryphal ones included in the Septuagint, the Greek translation of the Hebrew Bible completed in Alexandria, Egypt, about 250 B.C. The Apocrypha and other doubtful books of Scripture also showed up in the vast Dead Sea Scroll library discovered

Title page from a Hebrew-Latin Bible, 1546

A partial list of Apocryphal writings from The Holie Bible, Bishops' Version, 1572

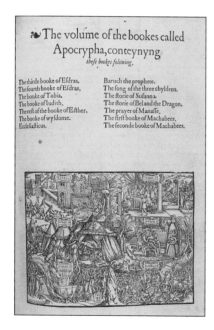

this century at Qumran, where the Essene sect had collected and studied Scripture between the second century B.C. and A.D. 70. The purpose of most of these Apocryphal books had been to round out the story of the Hebrew people and to bring it up to date, at least as far as the second century B.C.

BEGINNINGS OF THE CHRISTIAN CANON

The early Christian community held no meetings to discuss its canon, but first-century Christians did generally agree that certain Scriptural writings were acceptable and could be read aloud in church. They accepted the Jewish Scriptures as their own religious heritage and saw Jesus' mission as the fulfillment of the Messianic promises. After all, the Master himself had quoted the Hebrew Bible, as had Paul and the other apostles.

The earliest Christians also revered the teachings of Jesus that circulated in the oral tradition. Yet for many decades there wasn't any fixed canon of these teachings. And even after the four Gospels were written down, other accounts of Jesus' words and deeds continued to pass orally throughout the Roman Empire.

First-century Christians thought of the letters written by the Apostles Paul and Peter, or later in their names, as another element in their informal canon. Especially after the apostles were gone, earnest Christians combed these letters for inspiration and accepted their apostolic words as Holy Scripture. Christians weren't always sure, however, which letters had actually been written by the apostles.

"An Angel guideth Tobit," from The History of the Old and New Testament... *by the Sieur de Rotavmont, 1712*

REFINING THE CANON IN THE
SECOND CENTURY A.D.

Early in the second century, Christians read rather indiscriminately the enormous number of sacred writings in circulation. They agreed on the value of the four Gospels, as well as the writings of Paul, Peter, James, and John. But they also felt there was worth in some alternative versions of the gospel story—the Gospels of Truth, Philip, Hebrews, and Peter. And early church leaders had confidence in and quoted other Christian writings, including the Teaching of the Twelve Disciples; the Epistle of Barnabas; the Acts of Thomas, of Matthew, of Peter, of Paul; and several Apocalypses.

About midcentury, though, some zealous "heretics" forced church leaders to make their first serious effort toward forming a canon of Christian writings. One of these heretics was Marcion, a man who perhaps did not originally intend to part ways with the Church. He was a wealthy shipowner from Sinope, a city in present-day Turkey. He joined the church in Rome in about A.D. 140 but eventually rebelled against the orthodox theology of the Roman congregation and organized his own church. The Roman church excommunicated him in A.D. 144. But Marcion proceeded to win converts throughout the Roman Empire and organize them into communities.

Basically, Marcion saw Christianity as a gospel of love—totally excluding the Hebrew concept of law. In fact, he rejected the Hebrew Bible completely and felt that Paul alone of the New Testament writers fully understood the sharp differences between the Hebrew Law and Christian grace. So he put together his own body of Scripture, which included only ten letters of Paul and one Gospel, the book of Luke. And he edited these books dramatically—eliminating all references to Jewish law or tradition.

About the same time, another heretic, Montanus of Phrygia (also in modern-day Turkey), announced that the last days of Biblical prophecy had arrived. Claiming that he and his followers were the earthly representatives of the Holy Spirit, he wrote and circulated literature that he said was apostolic. Montanus—together with his two prophetesses, Maxmilla and Priscilla—traveled broadly with his message and his literature, sowing seeds of dissent in a number of Christian communities. It was this very dissent, however, that challenged church leaders to define both their creed and their Biblical canon.

EARLY ATTEMPTS AT A CHRISTIAN CANON

Marcion and Montanus—along with members of the Gnostic movement, which was producing its own brand of "heretical" literature—faced a number of orthodox opponents. Among them was Irenaeus, Bishop of Lyons, one of the first major Christian theologians.

Toward the end of the second century, Irenaeus made the first attempt at creating an official church canon. His main criterion for measuring the value of Christian books was their closeness to the apostles' message. On the basis of this standard, Irenaeus concluded that Matthew, Mark, Luke, and John were fully reliable. He felt, however, that there should be no more than four Gospels, since that number corresponded with the four winds. Other books he approved included the letters of Paul, I Peter, I John, the Revelation of John, the Shepherd of Hermas, and the Wisdom of Solomon. Excluded from his canon were the books of James and the Epistle to the Hebrews.

The scholar Origen was another early church leader who worked on the New Testament canon. Born in Alexandria, he grew up in a devout Christian household. When his father was killed during the persecution of Christians in Alexandria, it was all his mother could do to prevent Origen from seeking a martyr's death also. From that time forward—like many Christians of his time—he led a life of voluntary fasting and poverty, eventually traveling to Rome and Palestine, where he became a lay preacher. In A.D. 231, he founded a school in Caesarea and devoted himself to preaching and writing. In A.D. 250, during another persecution of Christians, he was imprisoned and brutally tortured until his death several years later.

Origen devoted his life to Bible scholarship, translating the early Christian texts into five languages. He was the first to give the name "New Testament" to Christian Scripture. He also refined the canon, dividing Christian writings into three categories: books he felt were canonical, those he felt must be rejected, and those that were questionable. If our present-day New Testament included only the material that Origen approved, it would have just twenty-two books—the four Gospels, Acts, fourteen letters of Paul, I Peter, I John, and Revelation.

THE CANON OF EUSEBIUS

Another great early reformer who influenced the Christian canon was Eusebius, longtime Bishop of Caesarea, the Roman capital of Palestine. Known as the Father of Church History, Eusebius wrote a ten-volume *Ecclesiastical History*, focusing on the Eastern Christian Church. He also wrote a number of other works on theology and Scripture, and attended the important ecumenical Council of Nicaea, held in A.D. 325 near present-day Istanbul. Emperor Constantine had called the council to meet a crisis in the Church—the spread of the "Arian" heresy about the relationship between Christ and God. The council condemned the heresy but agreed on a set of theological beliefs now known as the Nicene Creed—a creed still used in many churches today.

Educated by a student of Origen, Eusebius adopted Origen's three-category classification of Christian Scriptures. He also followed Origen in classifying as Apocryphal the Epistle of Barnabas, the Apocalypse of Peter, and the Wisdom of Solomon. He was doubtful about the Revelation of John and saw no value in the Shepherd of Hermas, a book Origen had placed in his disputed category. Eusebius was a staunch churchman till the end, enduring imprisonment and persecution for the cause of Christianity.

THE CHRISTIAN CANON FINALIZED

The early church leader who cemented the Christian canon in writing was Athanasius, Bishop of Alexandria for about forty-five years. As a young man, he too had attended the Council of Nicaea, which made an unforgettable impression on him. He devoted the rest of his life to defending passionately the orthodox Christian beliefs the council propounded—even though this meant he was sometimes hounded by secret police and had to spend some seventeen years in exile. In fact, most of his years as bishop were spent evading the plots of heretics who wanted to oust him.

Title page of the New Testament, Coverdale Bible, 1535

Athanasius, one of the greatest scholars of early Christianity, was a prolific writer. In addition to his theological works defending the Nicene Creed and attacking the Arian heresy, he wrote numerous works on Scripture. One of these, completed in A.D. 367, gave a new version of the Christian canon. It listed as authoritative all twenty-seven books that now make up our New Testament. These books, which Athanasius considered "springs of salvation," included not only the ones that Eusebius had accepted as reliable but also those that had been in Eusebius' "disputed" category.

From Athanasius' time forward, the New Testament canon was settled—at least in the Eastern Church. In A.D. 397, the Council of Carthage confirmed the canon for the Western Church.

Perhaps the most compelling reason the early Christians felt they needed a canon was to have a body of correct teaching that could defeat the onslaught of heresies threatening to dilute, or even destroy, pure Christianity. Also, after the Jews had decided on a Scriptural canon in the last decade of the first century A.D., the Christian community felt they needed their own body of literature–one focused on the teachings of Jesus and the mission of his Church. They felt, too, that Christian Scripture should spell out the differences between Judaism and Christianity, showing how Christianity had built a new and distinctive faith on the foundations of Judaism.

And what criteria did the early Christians use as they earnestly and prayerfully evaluated the maelstrom of Christian writings–both accurate and inaccurate–swirling around the Roman Empire? Generally, they felt that Holy Scripture should have been written by, or in some way connected with, the apostles. They felt, too, that the Scriptures quoted most often by the early Church Fathers had a special authority. But, most of all, they felt that Christian writings should be tested by a simple "rule of faith" (*regula fidei*). In other words, if a Gospel or epistle expressed the truths that these early Christians felt in their hearts were at the core of Jesus' teaching, then they accepted it as valid. If not, they rejected it.

So Athanasius' canon wasn't an arbitrary selection of books by a few church officials. It reflected the consensus of the whole Christian community, guided–as they felt sure they were–by the Holy Spirit. The canon was, in a sense, the *people's* choice. It contained those truths about God, Christ Jesus, and humanity which–in the first arduous centuries after Jesus' ministry–had proved most valuable as sources of inspiration and healing. It contained the Scriptures that best represented to early Christians the Word of God–the ones they wanted to pass down to truth-seekers in every age.

CHAPTER EIGHT

The Apocrypha: Historical Link between the Testaments

Hidden things," "mysterious or esoteric lore," "secret knowledge accessible only to an inner circle of believers"—all these expressions have been used to describe the Old and New Testament Apocrypha. Some of these Apocryphal books contain fascinating historical material. Others resemble the wisdom literature of the Old Testament. And still others read more like fables. Yet although there's been considerable interest in these books over the centuries, they haven't ultimately passed the test of "Scripture." One way or another, they've been found wanting and so have been excluded from the canon.

Today some Bible translations contain selections from the Apocryphal writings. But virtually no one accepts these writings as canon. Worshipers feel these books simply haven't proved themselves—in the way the accepted books of the Bible have—to be the Word of God.

One of the books in the Old Testament Apocrypha, II Esdras (another name for Ezra), explains the tradition behind the Apocrypha. In this book, Ezra relates how God spoke to him out of a bush and told him to write down words of understanding that He would give him. So Ezra called together five scribes, who recorded—over a period of forty days—ninety-four books filled with revelations from God. Of these books, according to II Esdras, God told Ezra to publish just twenty-four. The remaining seventy were to be given by Ezra only to the "wise among your people"—those who supposedly were spiritually qualified to partake of "the spring of understanding, the fountain of wisdom, and the river of knowledge" (II Esdras 14:46, 47). According to some interpretations of this passage, the twenty-four books correspond to the canonical Old Testament, while the seventy secret ones correspond to the Apocrypha.

Just what are these Apocryphal books, and where did they come from? Originally, they consisted of hundreds of writings, both Jewish and Christian. The Old Testament Apocrypha is made up of Jewish writings and the New Testament Apocrypha of Christian writings. For the most part, the Old Testament books were written between 400 B.C. and A.D. 250, and the New Testament books during the first few centuries after the birth of Jesus.

THE OLD TESTAMENT APOCRYPHA

Most of the books in the Old Testament Apocrypha were written during years of severe tribulation for the Jews—when the Greeks, and later the Romans, bore down on the children of Israel, pressuring them to give up their faith in the one God in favor of pagan gods and Hellenistic culture. So thinkers and writers during this period recorded historical accounts, novel-like stories, teaching material, prayers, letters, and apocalyptic visions that they thought might inspire and hearten their fellow Jews as they faced persecution and oppressive foreign rule.

It was the Jews originally brought as prisoners to Alexandria, Egypt, who first published the Apocrypha in the Greek version of the Hebrew Bible known as the Septuagint. This version, begun about 250 B.C., was quickly accepted not only by Alexandrian Jews but by Greek-speaking Jews throughout the Roman Empire.

An eighteenth-century print showing the port and city of Alexandria

The number of books included in the Old Testament Apocrypha differs in the various versions of the Judeo-Christian Scriptures, most of which contain either fourteen or fifteen books. Generally, these writings tell the story of a period in Jewish history that isn't covered in the canonical Old Testament—the tumultuous time between the late sixth century B.C. (when the priest Ezra led the Jews out of exile in Babylon) and the birth of Jesus. This time span includes the rebuilding of the Temple at Jerusalem, the conquest and cultural brainwashing of the Jews by Alexander of Macedon, and the tyranny of such despots as Antiochus Epiphanes (Antiochus IV, mentioned earlier), who demanded that the Jews worship him.

Although the Apocrypha was popular among the Jewish people, the rabbis ultimately rejected it from the Hebrew canon in the latter part of the first century A.D. In their eyes, these books didn't measure up as Scripture. And the close connection between the Apocryphal books and the Septuagint did nothing to make the Apocrypha any more credible with the rabbis, who looked askance at the Septuagint because it was written in Greek and not in Hebrew.

Neither Jesus nor the apostles quoted directly from the Apocrypha. And New Testament writers as a whole say almost nothing about the stories and historical events these books contain.

CHRISTIANS CONTINUE THE
APOCRYPHAL TRADITION

Interestingly enough, it was the Greek-speaking *Christians* who popularized the Old Testament Apocrypha. This may have been because most Christians used the Septuagint, which is quoted liberally in the New Testament. Even though the New Testament writers don't quote directly from the Old Testament Apocrypha, they do sometimes echo passages from these books.

Through the years, the use of the Apocrypha within Christianity has been a controversial affair. A number of the early Church Fathers, such as the great Bible scholar Origen, quoted the Apocrypha as authoritative Scripture, but they often came under fire for doing so. The Bishop of Emmaus, Julius Africanus, for instance, criticized Origen for quoting from the book of Susanna. And in the fourth century A.D., the most learned of the early Church Fathers, the Roman Catholic Bible scholar Jerome, for a long time refused to translate the Apocrypha into Latin when he was preparing his monumental Latin Vulgate Bible. But the Catholic bishops eventually succeeded in pressuring him into including the old Latin Apocrypha in his new Bible.

About the same time, the renowned church thinker Augustine signaled his approval of the Old Testament Apocrypha and urged that it be made part of the Biblical canon. Thanks to endorsements like this, the Apocrypha went on to enjoy *almost canonical status* during the entire Middle Ages.

THE REFORMATION CHALLENGE TO THE APOCRYPHA

With the coming of the Renaissance and the rebirth of Greek studies in the fifteenth century, scholars and church leaders began to question the trustworthiness of the Apocryphal books again. This was especially true after the fall of Constantinople in 1453, when leading Greek scholars fled from that city to Western Europe with their ancient Bible manuscripts. These texts inspired new, more accurate translations of the Bible into the common languages of the times and forced a reassessment of the Apocrypha.

When the reformer Martin Luther completed his revolutionary translation of the whole Bible—including the Apocrypha—into German in 1534, he shocked church authorities by stating in his foreword that the Apocryphal books should *not* be considered sacred Scripture, even though they are instructive. Then other Protestant Bible translators followed Luther's example by segregating the Apocrypha from the rest of the Scriptural text. So the Roman Catholic Church responded with a strong assertion at the Council of Trent, in 1546, that anyone who published a Bible *without* the Apocrypha would be excommunicated.

In 1599, some printers of the Geneva Bible, an English Bible translated by radical Protestants in Switzerland, omitted the Apocrypha altogether from certain printings of this Bible. But the first editions of the King James Bible, published in 1611, *included* the Old Testament Apocryphal writings, although they were separated from the canonical writings and sandwiched between the Old and New Testaments.

As early as 1616, however, certain radical printers began leaving the Apocrypha entirely out of the King James texts, even though the Archbishop of Canterbury threatened to imprison anyone who published the Bible without the Apocrypha.

Over the centuries the number of King James Bibles omitting the Apocryphal books eventually exceeded those which included them, until virtually none of these editions printed them. Finally, in 1826, the British and Foreign Bible Society decided to stop publishing the Apocrypha in any of its Bibles.

The Apocrypha included in 1611 King James Bible

THE SIGNIFICANCE AND INFLUENCE OF THE APOCRYPHA

The Old Testament Apocryphal books provide a historical bridge between the Old and New Testaments. They span the five-hundred-year hiatus that's not covered by the Old Testament. Even though some of the Apocryphal stories are fictional, they still tell much about this period that historians could discover in no other way. Some of the Old Testament Apocryphal books, for instance, paint a compelling picture of the heroic efforts of the Jewish people to maintain their faith in the face of political, military, and religious oppression under foreign rule. So, viewed as a multifaceted historical document, these writings offer a valuable backdrop for study of both Old and New Testaments.

Also, the Apocryphal books have influenced a number of religious, literary, and artistic works. For example, the works of Shakespeare contain roughly eighty references to the Apocrypha. Handel based his oratorios *Susanna* and *Judas Maccabaeus* on the Apocryphal books. And the nineteenth-century Russian pianist and composer Anton Rubinstein centered his opera *The Maccabees* on Apocryphal history.

THE EARLIEST APOCRYPHAL WRITINGS: STORIES AND LETTERS

Probably the oldest of the Apocryphal books is the book of **Tobit**. It's based on smatterings of ancient Jewish folklore that were woven into one story in the third century B.C. This book is a romantic tale of heartbreak, betrothal, marriage, reward, and healing for Tobit and his entire family, who lived righteous and God-fearing lives in exile in eighth-century B.C. Assyria. The story has a happy ending, but it's slow in coming, just as—the writer implies—Israel's final deliverance from oppression will be. The book of Tobit sends a strong message to third-century Jews living under foreign oppression: *Don't be fainthearted!* God will save and heal you if you simply trust Him and remain faithful to the Hebrew Law.

Written about the same time, or perhaps as late as the second century B.C., the **Letter of Jeremiah** is composed as if it's a message from the Old Testament prophet Jeremiah to the Jews exiled in Babylon in the late seventh or early sixth century B.C. The letter is a strongly worded attack on the idols of the Babylonians—much like that in the Old Testament book of Jeremiah—declaring that these gods are only material objects, with no life, power, or real identity of their own. "Like a scarecrow in a cucumber bed, which guards over nothing," the author writes, "so are their gods of wood, overlayed with gold and silver" (Letter of Jeremiah 6:70). As is the book of Tobit, the Letter of Jeremiah is really a message to the author's contemporaries, warning them not to worship other gods.

The author of the book of **Baruch** was, according to tradition, Jeremiah's secretary, who was writing from exile in Babylon to the Jerusalem Jews. The book is a collection of prayers and poems paraphrased from the Old Testament books of Daniel, Job, and Isaiah. These writings are strung together in four major sections: an introduction urging the Jews to be generous and to pray for the Babylonian emperor, a prayer of confession and petition for deliverance, a hymn addressed to personified Wisdom, and a beautiful prayer filled with reassuring statements like this: "Take courage, O Jerusalem, for the one who named you will comfort you. . . . The woods and every fragrant tree have shaded Israel at God's command" (Baruch 4:30; 5:8).

The brief book of **Susanna** is often thought of as one of the most charming stories in Jewish literature.

"The woods and every fragrant tree have shaded Israel at God's command" (Baruch 5:8)

Written in the third or second century B.C. and later bound in with the Septuagint's version of the book of Daniel, Susanna describes how a virtuous and beautiful young wife living in Babylon during the Exile–through her simple innocence and unquestioning trust in God–manages to triumph over a couple of wily and corrupt judges who try to blackmail her into granting them sexual favors. Just as Joseph refuses the advances of Potiphar's wife in the Old Testament, Susanna stands firm against the elderly judges, even though they try to destroy her reputation by accusing her of adultery.

Dragged into court and put on trial for her life, Susanna desperately prays to God, who sends Daniel to rescue her. During the trial, Daniel cross-examines the judges separately, proves them both to be liars, and vindicates Susanna. The judges are put to death, while Susanna's relatives rejoice and praise God. And, in the words of the author, "From that day on, Daniel was held in high regard" (Susanna 1:64). Like most of the other early Old Testament Apocryphal writings, the story of Susanna shows how important it is to obey the Hebrew Law, right down to the last detail, even under the heaviest pressure–even when your very life is at stake.

Illustration of Susanna and the judges from The History of the Old and New Testament... *by the Sieur de Rotavmont, 1712*

CHAPTER NINE

Later Old and New Testament Apocryphal Writings

SECOND-CENTURY B.C.
APOCRYPHAL WRITINGS

The second century before the birth of Jesus was a tempestuous period in Jewish history. A power struggle was under way in the Middle East. Ever since the death of Alexander the Great in 323 B.C., his eastern kingdom had been divided between the Ptolemies of Egypt and the Seleucids of Syria. At the beginning of the second century B.C., these two major dynasties were battling for control of Palestine. But eventually the Seleucids, who had enthusiastically embraced the Greek culture of Alexander, asserted their supremacy.

In an attempt to build political unity, the Seleucids tried to impose their Hellenized culture and religion on the Jews. By 175 B.C., when Antiochus Epiphanes (Antiochus IV) came to the throne in Syria, the pressure on Jews to conform to Greek traditions had reached a crisis point. Although some aristocrats cooperated with Antiochus, most Jews fiercely resisted the attempt at forced Hellenization. Antiochus reacted by revoking the religious rights of all Jews.

One family in particular, the Hasmoneans, led a tenacious guerrilla resistance against the forces of Antiochus. From their power base in the hills outside Jerusalem, these deeply religious rebels struck repeatedly at the enemy under the brilliant leadership of Judah the Maccabee (meaning "the Hammer" in Hebrew). Before he was killed in battle, Judah managed to free the Temple in Jerusalem. Then his brother Jonathan continued the fight, driving the Seleucids out of Palestine by 150 B.C. After Jonathan's death in captivity, the youngest Hasmonean brother, Simon, completed the victory over the Seleucids and finally reestablished free worship in Palestine. Thus began a century of independence for the Jews under Hasmonean rule.

It is natural that the Biblical and Apocryphal literature written during the second century B.C. would reflect the stress felt by the Jewish people as they fought their way to independence. Some of the Apocryphal books written in this century urge them to resist religious domination, as they had during the Babylonian Exile. Others celebrate the victories of the Hasmonean dynasty. Still others encourage the Jews to reconstruct their ancient traditions and religious lifestyle, as Ezra had done during the rebuilding of Jerusalem.

Illustration depicting Judas Maccabaeus from The History of the Old and New Testament... *by the Sieur de Rotavmont, 1712*

I Esdras, more than any other book in the Old Testament Apocrypha, is intertwined with the Bible itself. It's actually a rewrite—or perhaps an early version—of the Biblical story of the return of the Jews from Exile in Babylon in the late sixth century B.C. In the canonical Old Testament, this story appears in II Chronicles, Ezra, and Nehemiah.

The first book of Esdras includes an additional story describing a contest among three bodyguards of King Darius of Persia. Each is to say what he feels is "the strongest thing in the world." The winner is to become adviser to the king and receive marvelous gifts. One bodyguard argues that wine is the strongest thing in the world. Another says the king is strongest. The third—Zerubbabel, the crown prince of Judah—says that nothing exceeds the power of Truth. Zerubbabel wins the contest. The king is so impressed with his wisdom that he allows Zerubbabel to return home to rebuild Jerusalem.

The rest of I Esdras focuses on how Zerubbabel and Ezra lead the Jews back to Jerusalem—and freedom. They rebuild the Temple and reestablish the Law of God. Nehemiah's role in this rebuilding process, so prominent in our Bible, is virtually eliminated in I Esdras.

Another short piece of Apocryphal writing dating from the second century B.C. is **Psalm 151**, a musical poem retelling two events in King David's career: his selection as king by Saul, and his triumph over Goliath the Philistine. The speaker in the psalm is David, and his words echo the account in I Samuel 16 and 17.

Written about the same time as Psalm 151, **Bel and the Dragon** was originally in the Septuagint's book of Daniel. The story takes place in the Persian court of King Cyrus during the Jewish Exile

(Left) Illustration of Bel and the Dragon;
(Right) Illustration of Judith;
both from The Apocrypha, Embellished with Engravings, from Pictures and Designs by the most Eminent English Artists, *1816*

in Babylon. In it, Daniel is pressured to forsake the God of Israel and worship the Babylonian idols.

As the story opens, Cyrus is angry at Daniel because he won't worship the Babylonian god Bel. Although Bel is made of clay and bronze, Cyrus insists that he's a living god because he eats huge amounts of food each day. But Daniel manages to prove that the *priests,* and not Bel himself, are eating the food. Enraged, the king sentences the priests to death and allows Daniel to destroy both Bel and his temple.

Next, the king orders Daniel to worship a great dragon. But Daniel defies the king again and proves the dragon to be powerless by poisoning it. Outraged, the Babylonians demand that Daniel be thrown to the lions. Daniel spends six days in the lions' den, but he survives. The king is so impressed that he embraces the God of Israel.

Like so many of the other Apocryphal books written in the second century B.C., Bel and the Dragon rallies the Jews to fight back against religious oppression and mocks the worship of foreign gods.

The book of **Judith**, also written in the second century B.C., is even more militant about opposing foreign gods. Its main character is a beautiful and wealthy widow. Most Jewish readers of the period would have recognized immediately that Judith personifies Palestine. Her name represents both the ancient name Judah and Judah the Maccabee.

In this fictional story, the heroine learns that an Assyrian military conqueror named Holofernes is about to invade Palestine. After praying to God for help, she allows herself to be captured by the enemy and flatters Holofernes into thinking she is in love with him. When he becomes drunk one night, she kills him with his own sword. Then she returns home in triumph and the Assyrians flee.

This story must have been deeply heartening to the oppressed Jews of the period, showing that—with God's help—a defenseless nation and a courageous woman could withstand an overpowering military force.

Ecclesiasticus (the "church book"), also known as the **Wisdom of Jesus Son of Sirach**, is a collection of wise sayings, hymns, prayers, and general instructions for living. The book represents the teaching of a Jerusalem Jew named Jesus Ben Sira, who wrote down these sayings in the early part of the second century B.C. In the latter part of the century, Ben Sira's grandson moved to Alexandria and translated his grandfather's book into Greek for the Jewish community there.

This book is written in the tradition of the Bible's great wisdom literature—Proverbs, Ecclesiastes, and Job. The main argument of Ecclesiasticus is that, to be wise, a person has to fear God and live the spirit of the Torah, or Hebrew Law. "The fear of the Lord is the crown of wisdom, making peace and perfect health to flourish," Ben Sira writes (Sirach 1:18). As in Proverbs, Wisdom is personified as a woman. Her "Hymn of Praise" to herself is the centerpiece of the book.

Ecclesiasticus is filled with other, more human types of wisdom also: advice on family relationships, table manners, how to handle money, friendship, and the treatment of slaves. The last section of the book, a "Hymn in Honor of Our Ancestors," praises the early Hebrew patriarchs. Taken as a whole, Ecclesiasticus urges Jews not to abandon their Jewish heritage and to remain faithful to the Law of God which has brought them safely through so many trials.

The **Song of the Three Youths** is another addition to the Biblical book of Daniel. This short book was written about the middle of the second century B.C. It fills in details of the story of the three young

Hebrew men whom King Nebuchadnezzar of Babylon threw into the fiery furnace because they refused to worship idols. The book has three parts: the prayer of Azariah (Abednego) from the midst of the furnace, a short prose section telling how an angel cools down the flames with "a moist wind," and a song of praise by the three young men after they're delivered.

Azariah's prayer expresses not only his personal plea but a broader appeal to God for the deliverance of the whole Jewish nation from captivity. To mid-second-century Jews, this prayer would have been a plaintive cry for help as they faced the cruel persecution of Antiochus IV Epiphanes. The song the three young men sing at the end of the book leaves no doubt that earnest prayer for deliverance *is answered.*

I Maccabees, written at the end of the second century B.C., is an accurate account of the birth of the Hasmonean dynasty in Judea. It tells the story of the freedom struggle championed by Judah Maccabee and his brothers. The author of this account is convinced that the Hasmonean rebels were acting in accord with God's will. This book is written in the style of the Old Testament histories in Samuel and Kings, reflecting the theological view that God is ever-active in the political and military destiny of His people.

II Maccabees covers basically the same historical period as I Maccabees but was written a few decades later. It's considered less trustworthy than the earlier account, although it contains much more detail and is told far more dramatically. There are other differences, too. For instance, the focus in II Maccabees is on Judah alone as the leader of the Hasmonean resistance. His brothers Jonathan and Simon—so prominent in the earlier book—are barely mentioned.

Also, the author of II Maccabees is far more concerned with Antiochus' threat to the Temple than is the author of I Maccabees, who stresses the political and military aspects of the assault on Judea. At the beginning of the book, the author describes how two Jews— Jason and Menelaus—defile the Temple by using its treasures to buy the office of high priest for themselves. For this sin, God punishes the Jews by sending Antiochus to destroy the Temple. But because the Jews genuinely repent of their sins, God later sends Judah Maccabee to deliver them.

Another highly unusual feature of II Maccabees is its direct reference to the resurrection of the dead. Several of the martyrs in the book say they believe God will reward their faithfulness with life after death. As one of them cries out just before being killed, "One cannot but choose to die at the hands of mortals and to cherish the hope God gives of being raised again by him" (II Maccabees 7:14).

The Old Testament Apocrypha also includes the **Additions to Esther**, added to the Septuagint Old Testament at the end of the second century or the beginning of the first century B.C. The main purpose of these "additions" is to make the Biblical book of Esther–which never mentions the word *God*–seem more religious. So the six brief additions refer to God some fifty times in their one hundred and seven verses, and they include two prayers: one by Esther, the Jewish queen of Persia, and the other by her uncle Mordecai. Overall, the additions clarify that Esther's life, and the lives of her people, are preserved because of her religious ardor, and not just because of her beauty and bravery.

FIRST-CENTURY B.C. APOCRYPHA

Another Apocryphal book on the Maccabean conflict is **IV Maccabees**. Written between fifty and one hundred years later than I and II Maccabees, it was for many years thought to have been the work of the famous Jewish historian Josephus. The book differs from earlier accounts of the Maccabean revolt in this way: it sees that conflict from the standpoint of the Greek philosophy and rationalism that were so much a part of the Hellenistic period. Fourth Maccabees shows, for instance, how the Jewish martyrs overcame their fear of death through a combination of faith *and* reason.

This book begins by stating that "reason is the guide of the virtues, but over the emotions it is sovereign" (IV Maccabees 1:30). Then, the author proves his point by describing the courageous defiance shown by certain Jews who were put to death by Antiochus. The first of these is the elderly Hebrew leader Eleazar, who, just before being beaten to death, cries out to his fellow Jews, "O Children of Abraham, die nobly for your religion!" After that, the author gives a detailed description of the martyrdoms of seven Jewish brothers and their mother, all of whom rejoice in the opportunity to give their lives for their faith.

All these martyrs, however, end up safely in the presence of God, according to IV Maccabees, resurrected forever because of their virtue. Their martyrdom, the author implies, atones for Israel's sins and purges the nation of guilt.

Like the book of Proverbs in the Bible, the Apocryphal **Wisdom of Solomon** is written in the name of the ancient Israelite king famous for his spiritual understanding. The book is addressed to foreign kings, telling them how to manage their realms. However, most scholars think its message is actually aimed at the million or more Jews living under persecution in Alexandria in the last half of the first century B.C. The Wisdom of Solomon offers comfort to these Jews and argues that they should resist the allurements of pagan idolatry and stand by the ancient Mosaic Law.

Though we don't know exactly who the author of the Wisdom of Solomon was, it's clear from the format of his book—a long and complex poetic discourse full of scholarship and cast in the Greek philosophical mode—that he was a deeply religious Jewish intellectual. He was well schooled in Hellenism yet faithful to the basic Jewish tradition. He believed that Jews who withstand persecution in this life will have immortality in the next. On the other hand, the sinful oppressors of the righteous—even though they seem to flourish in this life—will meet severe judgment hereafter.

FIRST-CENTURY A.D. APOCRYPHA

The **Prayer of Manasseh** emphasizes God's merciful forgiveness of those who genuinely repent of their transgressions. Just fifteen verses long, the prayer focuses on Manasseh, the seventh-century B.C. king of Judah described in the Bible as a wicked monarch who forced the Jews to worship Baal and killed those who remained loyal to Yahweh. According to II Chronicles, Manasseh repented of his sins while he was in captivity in Babylon. And when he prayed humbly for forgiveness, God heard his petition and restored him to the throne. The Apocryphal prayer supplies what the author imagines might have been Manasseh's own words.

The prayer was probably written by someone who wanted to comfort those Jews who had adopted Hellenistic gods. Manasseh's earnest petition for forgiveness would have sent this message to Jews who had abandoned the faith: The "God of those who repent" is ready to pardon even the worst of sins, if the sinner is willing to give his whole heart to the Lord (Manasseh 1:13).

A short historical novel, **III Maccabees** has nothing to do with the Maccabean revolt but is so named because it comes right after II Maccabees in most versions of the Apocrypha. It centers on Ptolemy Philopator, king of Egypt in the late third century B.C. The book was written by an unknown Jew in Alexandria when his people were under heavy persecution in that city—possibly during the terrifying reign of the Roman emperor Caligula in the first century A.D.

The book opens with a description of how a Jew saves Ptolemy from being assassinated. Then the king—apparently forgetting that he owes his life to a Jew—tries to force his way into the Jerusalem Temple and is prevented by God's intervention. Infuriated, Ptolemy returns to Egypt and strips the Jews of their citizenship, coercing them into worshiping the Greek god Dionysus. When they refuse, he condemns them to be trampled to death by a herd of elephants. The prayers of the Jews prevent this disaster, and the elephants trample the *Egyptians* instead. Awed by this turn of events, Ptolemy immediately changes his policy toward the Jews and lets them return home unharmed. The story makes this point to the Alexandrian Jews: You don't have to be afraid. Your God is at hand to save you.

The last book to be added to the Old Testament Apocrypha— **II Esdras**—wasn't written until the end of the first century A.D., in the wake of the destruction of Jerusalem by the Romans in A.D. 70. The introduction and conclusion were added even later, possibly as late as the third century A.D. By this time, virtually all Jews had been expelled from their homeland, not to return for almost nineteen centuries. The author of II Esdras, probably one of the Jews in exile, is clearly struggling to cope with the tragedy his people have endured. For him, the best way to view this catastrophe is to see it in apocalyptic terms—as a sure sign that the last days are close at hand, when God will justify Israel and avenge her enemies.

The main section of II Esdras is a series of seven apocalyptic visions shown to Ezra, the high priest who reestablished the Torah among the Jews after their return from Exile in the fifth century B.C.

These visions come in response to intense questions that Ezra puts to the angel Uriel—questions that are more like complaints.

The final vision, as mentioned previously, tells how Ezra is called by God to receive a revelation of Scripture—some of which is to be made public and some to remain private. According to tradition, the twenty-four books of public revelation correspond to the Bible, while the seventy that remain private correspond to the Apocrypha. The book closes with a forecast of calamity for Israel's enemies and salvation for God's chosen people, the children of Israel.

EZRA: A KEY FIGURE IN THE OLD TESTAMENT APOCRYPHA

It's significant that both the first and the last book framing the Old Testament Apocrypha, I and II Esdras, focus on the high priest Ezra. In this sense, Ezra—the great rebuilder of Jerusalem and the reestablisher of her ancient Law—is a dominant figure in the Apocrypha. And this is understandable. These books were written between the second century B.C. and the third century A.D., when the Jewish people were under constant threat of cultural and religious extermination at the hands of the Hellenizers and later the Romans.

The Jews faced, too, an additional threat—the rise of splinter groups within Judaism. There were the Essenes, the Sadducees, and the Pharisees. And there was another group with ever-accelerating impact throughout the Mediterranean world, a group that built on the foundations of Judaism but wouldn't be kept within its bounds. It was grown into a full-blown movement by the late first century A.D.—a movement that would later be known as *Christianity*.

Confronted with all of this, the authors of the Old Testament Apocrypha looked for role models not so much to the ancient Hebrew patriarchs, as to Ezra, the man who had so successfully reconstructed their national religion and identity after the devastating Exile experience in Babylon. It's no coincidence that, according to II Esdras, Ezra is the prophet to whom God gave the sacred task of preserving the Scriptures for all time. His courage in the face of catastrophe, vision for the future of Palestine, and unswerving fidelity to the Law of God were all crucial to the survival of Jewish culture and religion.

In a sense, nearly all the heroes and heroines of the Apocrypha—Tobit, Daniel, Susanna, Judith, the Hasmoneans, Esther, and even the repentant infidel Manasseh—embodied the spiritual indomitability and stubborn grit of Ezra. If the Jews were ever to survive dispersal and persecution over the centuries, they'd surely have to hold close to their hearts all that Ezra stood for.

THE NEW TESTAMENT APOCRYPHA

No discussion about the Apocrypha would be complete without at least a brief summary of the New Testament Apocryphal writings. This enormous collection of material—poetry, prayers, dream sequences, liturgies, and fables—was created virtually all over Christendom, between the second and ninth centuries A.D.

Maybe it's easiest to think of the Apocryphal New Testament books as "shadow" versions (and notably unreliable ones!) of the canonical New Testament books. There are, for example, at least eleven well-known Apocryphal Gospels. The most prominent and reliable of these is the **Gospel of Thomas**, a collection of sayings and stories about the Master, supposedly dictated by Jesus to his "twin" brother, Judas Thomas. This gospel is strongly Gnostic in flavor, combining elements of myth, Greek philosophy, occultism, and Christianity.

The Gospel of Thomas contains a curious mix of stories about the young Jesus together with wise sayings collected from the Master's ministry. These boyhood tales bear little relevance at times to the traditional gospel story. On the one hand, they describe Jesus as a child able to perform wondrous deeds: controlling a rainstorm, making sparrows out of a mud puddle, healing a little boy who had hurt his foot, dazzling his schoolmaster with extraordinary knowledge, even raising the dead. Yet the gospel contains other material that seems preposterous, picturing Jesus as a child who would occasionally curse people who disagreed with him—or cause them to fall dead. Even in these cases, though, Jesus usually revived the dead people and blessed them.

Another Biblical type echoed in the New Testament Apocrypha is that of the "**Acts**." There are Acts supposedly written by or about Paul, Thomas, Peter, John, and other apostles. These contain special counsel for Christians as they go forward in their ministry. In the Acts of John, for example, the apostle tells his followers that Jesus Christ is still with them, even "in reproaches and insults, by sea and on dry land, in scourgings, condemnations, conspiracies, frauds, punishments." John goes on to promise, "If then ye abide in him, ye shall possess your soul indestructible."

The New Testament Apocrypha includes still other types of Biblical literature: "epistles" and "apocalypses" supposedly written by Peter, Paul, James, John, and Jesus' mother, Mary. The earliest of these, dating possibly from the end of the first century A.D., may have been rather trustworthy, since they were written so soon after Jesus and the apostles had completed their careers. Yet the latest New Testament Apocryphal texts—written in languages like Slavonic, Arabic, Coptic, and Anglo-Saxon—were largely fictional.

So exactly what is the value of the New Testament Apocrypha to us now? Simply this: It offers a valid and engaging record of the worship and holiness of centuries of earnest Christians. These Christians endeavored—against overwhelming odds of superstition, ignorance, and indifference—to hold on to their faith and pass it along to future generations. They didn't have the complete New Testament we do. And New Testament canon wasn't clearly established for them as it is for us. So they can hardly be blamed for not knowing the difference between reliable and unreliable "New Testament" manuscripts.

Christians in the far-flung outposts of a feudal world were grateful for *any* stories about the Master and his apostles. They couldn't always afford to be choosy. So telling and retelling the ancient New Testament stories, however imaginatively and inaccurately, was their valiant effort to make sure the flame of Christianity never went out. The New Testament Apocryphal writings were their attempts to refuel that flame in their own hearts and in those of their descendants down through the centuries.

loqui: sublimia glīantes. Recedāt vetera
de ore vestro: quia de⁹ scientiaꝛ dūs est: ꝛ
ipi ꝓparant cogitacōnes. Arꝰs fortiū su=
peratus est: et infirmi accīncti sunt roboꝛe,
Repleti pꝰs pro panibꝫ se locauerūt: et
famelici saturati sūt. Donec sterilis pepit
plurimos: et que mꝉtos habebat filios in=
firmata est. Dūs moꝛtificat et viuificat:
deducit ad inferos ꝛ reducit. Dūs pauperē
facit ꝛ ditat: humiliat ꝛ sublimat. Susci=
tans de puluere egenū: et de stercoꝛe erigens
pauperē. Ut sedeat cū principibꝫ: et soliū
gloꝛie teneat. Dūi enim sunt cardines ter=
re: et posuit sup eos oꝛbem. Pedes sctoꝛ
suoꝛū seruabit: ꝛ impy in tenebris contice=
scent: quia nō in foꝛtitudine sua roboꝛabiꞇ
vir. Dūm foꝛmidabūt aduersary eius: et
sup ipsos in celis tonabit. Dūs iudicabit
fines terre: et dabit imperium regi suo: et
sublimabit coꝛnu cristi sui. Gloꝛia patri. ā

V
THE LATIN
VULGATE
BIBLE:
AN IDEAL
THAT
WAS LOST

CHAPTER TEN

Jerome Brings the Hebrew Bible to the Western World

The great Bible scholar and translator Jerome was an early Church Father and the most learned man of his age. He was also a man of contradictions—generous and affectionate toward his friends yet merciless with his enemies, passionate about the causes he championed yet dedicated to an ascetic life that made him deny all passions, devoted to the woman who was his partner and spiritual support yet committed to a life of celibacy. But the driving motive behind his lifework was his single-minded determination to dig out Bible truth and preserve it for all time.

JEROME'S EARLY LIFE

Born around A.D. 347 in the town of Stridon on the northeast coast of what is now Italy, Jerome came from a wealthy family. When he was twelve, his parents sent him to Rome, where he studied Latin and Greek as well as rhetoric, grammar, and liberal arts under the famous grammarian Donatus. It was at this point that he developed a taste for the Latin classics—especially the prose and poetic works of Virgil, Cicero, and Seneca. But he also learned in Rome to love more deeply the Christian faith he had been raised in, and to feel more keenly his duty to God. At age nineteen he was baptized into the faith.

For the next twenty years, Jerome traveled widely. From Rome, he journeyed to Trèves in France, where he was swept up with the asceticism and monasticism that thrived there. Then he returned home to Stridon and linked up with a group of intellectuals in neighboring Aquileia who were practicing an ascetic lifestyle of fasting and penance.

After breaking with this group two or three years later, Jerome set out on an extensive journey through Thrace, Pontus, Bithynia, Galatia, and other areas of what is now Turkey, eventually arriving—exhausted and seriously ill—in Antioch. During his illness, he dreamed that he was arraigned before the judgment seat of Christ. When Jerome said that he was a Christian, Christ said, "Thou liest. Thou art a Ciceronian." This revelation so jolted Jerome that he vowed never again to study the classic "pagan" literature of the Latin writers. From that day forward, he devoted himself exclusively to his Biblical mission, armed with his nearly unique knowledge of Latin, Greek, and Hebrew.

THE DESERT YEARS

Jerome's dream, and his encounter with a desert monk named Malchus, caused him to withdraw for several years to the barren desert of Chalcis in Syria to live the strictest kind of ascetic life. During this time, he suffered terribly from loneliness and harsh conditions— living in a cave, sleeping on the ground, and wearing a garment made of coarse sackcloth.

Writing to a friend in later years, Jerome described his grueling ordeal this way: "In the remotest part of a wild stony desert, burnt up with the heat of the scorching sun so that it frightens even the monks that inhabit it, . . . I tamed my flesh by fasting whole weeks." His solitude, however, gave Jerome the opportunity to perfect his knowledge of Hebrew by studying with a converted Jew. This study was a labor of love, since virtually no Latin-speaking Christians knew Hebrew at that time, and there were no Hebrew grammar books or guides available.

The desert years ended unhappily, with Jerome at the center of a dispute in nearby Antioch and accused of being a heretic. Yet he never forgot the piety and spirituality of the monks he'd met in the desert, and he later wrote several volumes describing their lives and good works. In one of these he writes, "I have seen many fathers there who were living the lives of angels, and were fashioning their lives into the similitude of that of the Redeemer," healing the sick and working miracles.

After his sojourn in the desert, Jerome returned to Antioch, where Bishop Paulinus ordained him a priest in 378. Jerome accepted this office only on the condition that he would not have to assume the responsibilities of priest in a parish church. In that way he could continue his work as a monk and Bible scholar. During this time, Jerome attended lectures on the Scriptures given by Apollinarius,

Bishop of nearby Laodicea. These lectures were given in Greek, a language which Jerome continued to study during his stay in Antioch.

In pursuit of further Biblical knowledge, Jerome traveled to Constantinople, where Bishop Gregory of Nazianzus supervised his study for several years. Under Gregory's influence, Jerome translated, from Greek to Latin (the almost universal language of the whole former Roman Empire), fourteen Biblical homilies (short sermons focusing on a Bible passage) of the third-century scholar Origen as well as the *Chronicles* of Eusebius.

THE RETURN TO ROME

In 382, Gregory retired and Jerome returned to Rome. Pope Damasus, recognizing his talents as a scholar and linguist, made Jerome his secretary. At Damasus' request, Jerome wrote several pieces of Bible criticism and translated two sermons of Origen on the Song of Solomon. Then, urged on by Damasus, Jerome undertook a revision of the Old Latin version of the Gospels, based on the best available Greek manuscripts. He also updated the Old Latin Psalms, correcting that text with the Greek Septuagint.

This work established the direction of Jerome's lifetime career as a Bible scholar and translator. And it was at this time that he grew to understand the critical need for an accurate standard version of the Latin Bible to replace the many unreliable versions circulating. Not only were these informal Latin texts undignified and sometimes inaccurate, but they were based on the Septuagint and other texts that Jerome felt were inferior. He was convinced that only a return to the ancient Greek and Hebrew manuscripts would ensure that the new Latin text reflected the true Word of God.

From The Greek New Testament with the Vulgar Latin Translation of the Greek Text Inserted Between the Lines..., *1609*

Along with his work as a Bible translator, Jerome preached asceticism to a loyal following of wealthy and aristocratic Roman widows and young women. Among his students were some of the most prominent and dedicated women in

the early Church—Marcella and her sister Albina, Melania the Elder, and Paula, with her two daughters Blesilla and Eustochium. This close-knit coterie of holy-minded ascetics was offended by what they saw as the excesses of some of the Roman monks and clergy, and publicly denounced them for their moral laxity.

Not too surprisingly, Jerome made a number of enemies among the Roman Christians, who resented his accusations, as well as his rejection of the Septuagint and the Old Latin Bible. After the death of Jerome's patron Damasus in 384, there was no one to protect him and his followers from public furor. So in 385 he and his closest disciple, Paula—along with several other women in the group—set out on a pilgrimage to the Holy Land.

JOURNEY TO BETHLEHEM

Jerome and his followers spent the next year touring archaeological sites where the events recorded in the Bible had unfolded—particularly in Palestine and Egypt. In Alexandria, Jerome studied under the Bible scholar Didymus. He did this to gain a clearer insight into the Hebrew mind and to learn all he could from the methods of Bible interpretation used by the scholars in Alexandria, in Antioch, and in the Hebrew rabbinical tradition.

Finally, Jerome, along with Paula and her nunlike group of followers, settled in Bethlehem, the birthplace of Jesus. They quickly set about building, with Paula's financial backing, a double monastery for both men and women, as well as a hospice for visiting pilgrims. They were determined that there would never again be "no room in the inn" in Bethlehem, as there had been at the time of Jesus' birth.

Jerome took charge of the men's monastery, while Paula took on the spiritual care of the women's cloisters. Jerome also opened a school for boys, where they could receive a Bible-based education. During the thirty-four years of his stay in Bethlehem, Jerome gave almost daily spiritual instruction to the monks and his other followers. Often he spoke in homilies, such as the one he wrote on Psalm 91, where he interpreted the line "the Lord . . . is my refuge" this way: "My refuge, my God. . . . You alone are refuge; there are many wounds, but You only are physician."

LAUNCHING THE OLD TESTAMENT TRANSLATION

In 390, Jerome—inspired by Paula and her daughter Eustochium—embarked on his most challenging undertaking: the translation of the Hebrew Old Testament into contemporary Latin. He had been intensively preparing himself for the past decade to take on this arduous work.

Now Jerome was ready to announce publicly that he no longer had confidence in the Septuagint, the Bible version that Christians had always revered and the Greek version from which the Old Latin translation had come. To most Christians, including the theologian Augustine of Hippo, repudiating the Septuagint and the Old Latin texts in favor of a return to "Hebrew truth" seemed downright blasphemous—like denying the Word of God.

But, convinced he was right in returning to the ancient Hebrew original as the most trustworthy version of all, Jerome withstood the storm of protest he'd stirred up and proceeded with his fresh-from-the-Hebrew translation. He also took a strong and rather revolutionary stand for the Hebrew canon, which excluded all the Apocryphal books that many Christians had been enjoying for centuries—highly popular books like Judith and Tobit and the Wisdom of Solomon. Jerome was tired, he explained, of having to justify to Jewish Bible scholars in Palestine the Church's stubborn loyalty to a text and a canon that were flawed in so many ways.

It took Jerome some fifteen years to complete his monumental Bible translation. Scholars disagree as to which books he started with. Some think Job was his first book; others think he started with Samuel or Kings. In any case, the first books Jerome turned out were really revisions of the Old Latin text. His method of revision was to compare the Old Latin wording with Origen's *Hexapla*, which featured four versions of the ancient Hebrew text. His revision of the book of Job turned out to be radically different from the Old Latin. It was a fifth longer and far more faithful to the Hebrew original. And Jerome's revisions of Proverbs, Ecclesiastes, the Song of Solomon, and Chronicles—all among the first books he produced—are also quite different from the Old Latin.

But when Jerome began working on Isaiah and the major prophets, he stopped his practice of merely revising the Old Latin version. From that point forward, he forged ahead with a totally *new* translation—one that was highly accurate, lyrical, and beautiful. Far from backing down when his critics vented their hatred on him, Jerome seemed to draw a quiet kind of strength from meeting their resistance.

He persevered in his mission, toiling relentlessly. A pilgrim named Postumianus wrote about him: "He is always completely engrossed in his reading and his books. He never rests, day or night. He is reading or writing the whole time."

A FINAL CHALLENGE

When Jerome was within reach of his goal of completing his translation of the Old Testament, he suffered a great blow with the death of Paula in early 404. For almost twenty years the two had worked side by side to care for the spiritual needs of the ascetic community, first in Rome and later in Bethlehem. Jerome was devastated, unable to work for months.

But Paula's daughter Eustochium was soon able to take her mother's place as head of the women's cloister and as Jerome's confidante. And just as Jerome had dedicated many of his greatest works to Paula, he now dedicated most of his remaining achievements to Eustochium. With her support, Jerome moved forward to complete his monumental translation in 405–6.

Spine of The Greek New Testament with the Vulgar Latin Translation of the Greek…, *1609*

Jerome's labor produced an Old Testament that not only is faithful to its Hebrew original but also reflects the melodic Hebraic rhythms and style. He believed in word-for-word translation but wasn't afraid to depart from the original to make the sense of a passage more clear. For him, it was more important to communicate the *meaning,* or essence, of a passage than to give a literal rendering. And in the interest of what he called "grace" or "euphony," Jerome often substituted his own wording, especially when the Hebrew repeated a word or phrase numerous times. Inevitably, Jerome's own classic Latin style crept into his wording. In fact, scholars have noted that some passages in his Bible sound more like the Latin poet Virgil than the Hebrew prophets.

Jerome's translation of the Bible has had its critics down through the years. Some have said that he added too much of his own phrasing to the text and took too many liberties with the Hebrew original. Others have pointed out that he added too definite a Christian slant to the Old Testament. But most readers have admired Jerome's style, which always highlighted *content* rather than form and which

communicated Bible truth in simple, clear wording that anyone—
even the "vulgar" or uneducated—could understand. And because this
version of the Bible was so readily understood by Latin-speaking
churchgoers from all backgrounds, it became known as the Bible of
the people, or the "Vulgate" Bible.

After Jerome completed his translation of the Old Testament
in 406—and actually while he was still working on it—he turned out
several commentaries. The finest of these centered on the books of
Nahum, Habakkuk, Daniel, Isaiah, Ezekiel, Jeremiah, and Psalms. In
each of these commentaries, Jerome returned to the Hebrew text and
sometimes to the Septuagint as the basis for his Scriptural exposition.
This method of exegesis sent a clear message to Christians: It's impossible to understand the Old Testament without consulting the Hebrew
original, *and* it's impossible to understand the *New* Testament without
being a thorough student of the Old Testament.

In time (probably after Jerome's death), the magnificent Old
Testament translations he completed in Bethlehem were united with
his earlier Psalter and his revision of the Gospels. And the remainder
of the New Testament—a revision of the Old Latin text—was probably
the work of another translator. All this added up to a complete Bible,
the Vulgate, which served as Christianity's key version of Scripture for
the next thousand years.

Jerome's Old Testament was a text that could stand the
scrutiny of the most critical Jewish Bible scholars. Its fidelity to the
original Hebrew text and canon, as well as its undeniable beauty,
gave the Old Testament for the first time real credibility in the eyes of
Western Christendom.

At the end of his long life, Jerome was in some ways a broken man—grieving the recent passing of Eustochium, battling heresy
within the Church, and distraught over the impending fall of the
Roman Empire. But he must have felt deeply satisfied that he had
vastly improved Christianity's understanding of Biblical truth. And
through his translation and ardent defense of the Old Testament,
Jerome saved Western Christendom from losing its connection with
the Hebrew Bible.

CHAPTER ELEVEN

The Middle Ages: The Bible on Hold for a Thousand Years

A WORD ABOUT THE MIDDLE AGES

Most of us romanticize the Middle Ages. We picture knights of King Arthur's Round Table, castles, lords and ladies, wandering minstrels, and crusades to liberate the Holy Land. But these images weren't created until the last part of the medieval period. Actually, most of the Middle Ages in Western Europe—some eight hundred years of it—was a period of spiritual and cultural twilight. Some have even called it a time of political and cultural disintegration. Yet the medieval years were something else as well. They were a time of almost universal fidelity to the Christian ideal—and of determination to preserve that ideal in the face of almost insuperable odds.

In the fourth and fifth centuries, Germanic tribes from the north of Europe invaded the western Roman Empire and, bit by bit, brought down the great imperial state, turning it into a collection of feudal kingdoms. The brilliant civilization that the Roman Empire once had been gradually crumbled. What followed was, for most people, a time of shadowy ignorance. But there were islands of intellectual and spiritual light—the monasteries and the great universities that sprang up at Oxford and Salamanca and Paris, for instance. It was these institutions that kept alive the fires of learning during the medieval period. It was these islands of light that preserved Biblical truth for future ages.

THE LOSS OF PRIMITIVE CHRISTIANITY— AND THE BIBLE

By the close of the second century A.D., classical civilization had come to an end. The Roman Empire was on the decline—weakened by corruption, economic disintegration, and the ever-present threat of barbarian invasion. The emperors became more despotic than ever—imposing military conscription and heavy taxes. And they persecuted Christians periodically, as they had almost from the beginning.

But by the fourth century, the reign of the Roman emperor Constantine signaled a dramatic shift in the relationship between Christianity and the state. The night before a major battle against his rival Maxentius, a vision told Constantine (who had always worshiped the sun god) to put a *Christian* monogram on his soldiers' shields. When he won the battle the next day, his attitude toward Christianity changed forever. He began giving Christians special favors, restored their property, and granted them religious freedom. At the end of his life, Constantine himself was baptized a Christian.

Constantine's support gave the Church new strength. But it also introduced long-term problems for Christianity, particularly when he moved his capital from Rome to Byzantium, which he renamed Constantinople in his own honor. This move created a power vacuum in Rome—a vacuum quickly filled by a strong line of popes, who created a kind of "papal monarchy."

Throughout the Middle Ages, this papacy was the ruling authority to which all Western Christendom was subject. The popes assumed not only religious but also secular control over much of the old Roman world. For all practical purposes, the Church of the Middle Ages was a *church-state*—with absolute power to levy taxes, call up armies, make laws, and punish citizens who violated its laws. Yet this strong line of popes also provided an organizing principle for the West—one that ultimately helped preserve the Christian way of life.

With this Christianization of the Roman Empire (which Jerome and others saw as secularization of the Church), Bible study diminished dramatically. Over the centuries, the doctrinal teachings of the Church tended to replace the Bible in the hearts of Christians. And, as people gradually lost touch with the Scriptures, they moved away from certain early Christian practices—such as reading the Bible aloud in church services, preaching the gospel story in an evangelical manner, and practicing spiritual healing. At the same time, the actual text of the Bible became corrupted.

CORRUPTION OF THE LATIN VULGATE BIBLE

Jerome's translation of the Bible—completed in the early fifth century—was a far better text than the jumbled "Old Latin" Bible that preceded it. Yet, for a couple of centuries, the Roman world resisted the Vulgate, clinging to the Old Latin text as somehow purer and holier. For this reason, people insisted on changing, or "corrupting," the Vulgate as it fanned out from Italy and southern France into Germany, Ireland, England, and Spain. Some scribes, as they recopied the Vulgate, inserted the familiar Old Latin wording into Jerome's text because they liked it better. Others continued to use the Old Latin text as their base but inserted in it some of Jerome's passages.

It was this unstable situation that made the Roman author and monk Cassiodorus try to standardize the Vulgate text in the sixth century. He turned out a new Bible that stayed as close as possible to Jerome's original wording and the ancient Hebrew Scripture.

Unfortunately, though, this improved version of the Vulgate wasn't popular. Instead, *another* text that Cassiodorus produced—one that was far inferior—ended up having wide circulation. In fact, the British abbot Ceolfrid took it with him to England in the early eighth century. There it was recopied—with all its mistakes—into still another manuscript known as the *Codex Amiatinus*. And in that form it found its way to monasteries all over Europe.

The Vulgate was also badly corrupted in Spain. Jerome himself had given his text to some Spanish scribes who had come to Jerusalem to copy his Bible in 398. But the texts they copied didn't include some of Jerome's last and best revisions. Jerome may have sent these revisions on to Spain later, but they were never incorporated into the Vulgate text there. So, over the next two centuries, the Spanish Vulgate drifted even further from Jerome's original. Eventually, so many flawed texts were circulating in Spain that it was hard to tell which ones were reliable.

CHARLEMAGNE TRIES TO REFORM THE VULGATE

During the reign of the Frankish king Charlemagne, nearly every major monastery in Europe had an Irish monk-in-residence to guide its Bible studies. (The Irish monasteries specialized in Greek and Hebrew studies.) Charlemagne strongly supported this, since he felt that improving the Bible text would bring order and culture to his vast kingdom.

Encouraged by the king, two major scholars devoted their talents to correcting the Vulgate. The first was Theodulf, Bishop of Orléans

King Charlemagne

and one of the most brilliant theologians of the Frankish Empire. Under Charlemagne's patronage, Theodulf turned out several exquisitely illuminated manuscripts of the Vulgate. The other Bible scholar who worked to revise the Vulgate during Charlemagne's reign was the king's long-time religious adviser, Alcuin. Born and educated at York, in Britain, he met Charlemagne in 781 and soon became the king's royal tutor and abbot of Tours in France. Charlemagne commissioned Alcuin to revise both the Old and New Testaments.

Using texts he'd brought with him from England, Alcuin trained the monks under his supervision to correct errors in grammar and punctuation, and to return to Jerome's original wording. He produced a number of single-volume Bibles, many of which were ornately decorated. But these were filled with Alcuin's marginal comments, all of which explained the theology of the Church Fathers. Then later scholars incorporated his comments *into the Bible text.* This corrupted the Vulgate even further.

SCHOLASTICISM ALTERS JEROME'S BIBLE

In the twelfth century, a book by Peter Lombard, an Italian scholar, inadvertently caused more corruption of the Vulgate. Lombard's book, *The Sentences,* contained four volumes of teaching on theological subjects like the Trinity and the Sacraments. But the most striking thing about the book was its heavy quotation from the Church Fathers and its use of a complex method of theological reasoning that came to be known as "scholasticism." Eventually, this highly orthodox book became the standard statement of theology for the Catholic Church during the Middle Ages.

Tragically, scholars in Paris interwove Lombard's scholastic commentary into a new edition of Alcuin's Bible in the early thirteenth century. The result was the "Paris Bible," an edition with layer upon layer of scholastic theology built into the text. Students at the University of Paris soon disseminated this new one-volume Bible all over Europe.

By the early fourteenth century, the condition of Jerome's Vulgate was deplorable. Yet the seriousness of this situation was known only to the most elite scholars—those who had some knowledge of Latin, Greek, and Hebrew. The vast majority of lay citizens couldn't understand these languages. And they couldn't understand the Latin Bible either, since the Latin language had died out hundreds of years earlier. Gradually, a family of new—"vernacular"—languages became the means of day-to-day spoken communication.

NEW POPULAR LANGUAGES

The new vernacular tongues included the modern languages we use now in Western civilization: Romance languages like French, Spanish, Portuguese, and Italian; and Germanic languages like German and English. The important thing as far as the Bible is concerned, though, is that people who spoke these new languages in the Middle Ages were usually *totally out of touch* with Latin and with the Latin Bible that the Church maintained as its only official text—the one and only version of Scripture to be used in services or to be read by the clergy.

It's only fair to say that illiteracy prevailed among all but the monks, a few priests, and the nobility. But even if the common people *had* known how to read, the Church forbade them to read the Bible. The clergy felt it would profane the Scriptures to put them into common languages that *anyone* could understand—languages they believed weren't worthy of communicating the Word of God. Latin, they felt, was the only holy language.

At the height of its power in the early thirteenth century, therefore, the Church virtually shut down any possibilities for the average person to become familiar with the Scriptures. In most countries, this made it illegal for lay members even to *own* a Bible, much less read one.

Most church officials, however, felt they *were* giving the Bible to the people—at least to the extent that the people were able to understand it. But they were convinced that the people *couldn't* understand the Bible text without help from the clergy. They felt it was the office of the Church to interpret the Bible for the people—to give it to them in a simple form that illiterate individuals could understand. They pointed to the "people's Bible"—the medieval tradition of presenting

Bible stories in lively art forms—as the kind of interpretation the Church could provide. These art forms ranged from frescoes on the walls of the catacombs in Rome through wall paintings in the churches to jewel-like stained-glass windows and brilliantly illuminated manuscripts.

THE BIBLE BEGINS TO REACH THE PEOPLE

It would be the task of the great heroes and heroines of the Reformation to give the people the actual text of the Bible in ordinary spoken languages. And once the Bible was finally available in vernacular tongues, this provided a driving incentive for common men and women to learn to read. Even during the Middle Ages, though, a few fearless innovators gave the people *portions* of the Bible in language they could understand.

Illuminated page from the Tickhill Psalter, *a Gothic manuscript of medieval England, ca. 1310, depicting the Tree of Jesse*

THE EARLY GOTHIC BIBLE

One of the first reformers to give the Bible to his people in their native tongue was the Gothic king Ulfilas in the fourth century. Born of a Gothic father and a Christian mother from Cappadocia (in what's now Turkey), Ulfilas studied Greek and Latin, as well as Gothic, in his early education. As a young man, he became involved in Christian missionary work. Later he was made a bishop. Often called the "Apostle of the Goths," Ulfilas eventually translated most of the Byzantine Greek Bible into the Gothic language. His Bible is the only major work of literature left from the Gothic civilization.

THE ANGLO-SAXON AND ENGLISH BIBLES

The one Bible the Anglo-Saxon people knew about—and their contact with it was only indirect—was the Latin Vulgate text that missionaries like Augustine and Ceolfrid brought to England from Rome in the early seventh and eighth centuries. Yet only the monks had *direct* contact with these manuscripts, and most of them couldn't read Latin.

The story of the English vernacular Bible actually begins in the late seventh century with Caedmon, the first Anglo-Saxon Christian poet. A cowherd with the monastery in the Whitby area, Caedmon saw an angel one night who told him to write a song about creation. The next morning, according to legend, he found that he could—for the first time in his life—write exquisite lines of poetry in the complicated Anglo-Saxon verse forms that were popular in England at that time.

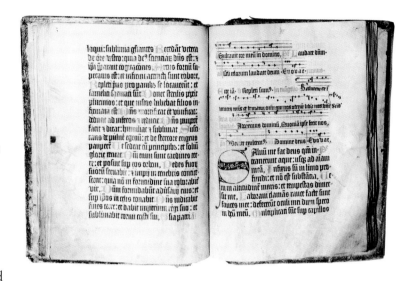

Fifteenth-century Mainz Psalter—the Book of Psalms—in Latin

After he finished his hymn on creation, Caedmon (or someone writing in his name) wrote a whole series of poems retelling Bible stories from Genesis, Exodus, and Daniel, as well as from the Gospels. These pieces sing with prophetic and mystical inspiration, but they wander far from the Bible itself.

Later, in the ninth century, the Midland poet Cynewulf told the story of Jesus' crucifixion in an even freer and more imaginative way than Caedmon had. And about that time, King Alfred the Great of Wessex sponsored a revival of learning that included translating parts of the Bible into Anglo-Saxon. According to tradition, the king himself began the translation of Psalms just before his death. But Alfred's translations were only for the clergy and the nobility. He never wanted ordinary people to read them.

It took the priest and writer Aelfric—in the tenth century—to finally give the common people large chunks of the Bible. Inspired by his patron, Earl Ethelweard, Aelfric wrote a lively series of sermons filled with Bible quotations—all translated into good, clear Anglo-Saxon. And, with Ethelweard's sponsorship, Aelfric put these sermons, as well as the Pentateuch, into book form so other priests could use them.

But Aelfric was a reluctant pioneer. He refused to translate the Gospels into English, fearing reprisals from the Church. He told Ethelweard in the preface to his translation of Genesis, "I dare not and I will not translate any book of the Bible after this book." Fortunately,

another Bible scholar (one who managed to remain anonymous) did
dare to put the Gospels into English during Aelfric's lifetime. This
translation, known as the *West-Saxon Gospels*, was never used in church
services and had to be circulated privately. But it finally gave people
the entire gospel story in their native tongue.

With the French Norman invasion of 1066 came an enormous
setback for the infant English Bible. As the Normans swept across the
land, they took over the monasteries and other centers of learning,
imposing French and Latin as the dominant languages.

About this time, an irrepressible strain began to develop in
English thought. It was an ardent desire—especially among women
and unlettered people with no opportunity to learn Latin—to *read the
Bible in their native language.* Quietly but inexorably, this group of prayer-
minded Christians grew. Eventually, in the fourteenth century, the
fervor of these English men and women boiled over into strident
expression. And in the last decades of that century, this movement of
the common people found its first great champion in an Oxford professor named John Wycliffe.

EARLY EUROPEAN BIBLES

Running parallel to the development of a people's Bible in England
were similar movements in Germany, the Low Countries, France, Italy,
and Spain. In Germany, for instance, the first vernacular Psalters came
in the ninth and tenth centuries, in the wake of Charlemagne's renaissance of learning. These appeared in a variety of dialects. Then, in the
late tenth and early eleventh centuries, a monastic schoolmaster
named Notker turned out fine German translations of the Psalter
and the book of Job in a burst of affection for the newly developing
German language.

In southern France, in the twelfth century, Peter Valdès, or
Waldo, a well-to-do merchant with a passion for Bible reading, gave all
his possessions to charity and launched a career as a preacher to the
poor people of Lyons. Furious about the Church's restrictions on Bible
reading, Valdès commissioned a translation of the New Testament
into the Provençal language. Then he gave this text to the people
through his followers, all of whom were "poor" preachers like himself.

When the pope told these "Waldensians" to stop preaching and handing out Bibles, Valdès retorted that he had to obey God—not man. The Church excommunicated him in 1184.

Valdès' followers branched out all over Europe and waged an underground campaign to give the Bible to the people. Eventually, the Waldensians—together with some related sects in Germany, Italy, and France—became the targets of a major inquisition by the Church. Dominican and Franciscan inquisitors traveled around Europe interrogating members of these Bible-reading sects and bringing them to trial for violating church prohibitions against studying Scripture, as well as for other forms of heresy. The Waldensians who were able to escape took refuge in the valleys of Italy, France, Spain, and Germany.

In each of these countries, people influenced by the Waldensians joined together in the thirteenth and fourteenth centuries to demand complete Bibles in their own languages. The Vulgate, many people knew, had become hopelessly corrupt and was incomprehensible to a public that couldn't understand Latin. But, more important, vernacular languages now had enough fluidity, precision, breadth of word choice, and beauty to support great and memorable versions of Scripture.

Outstanding scholars, poets, and writers were exuberantly pushing the limits of their vernacular languages. So it was natural that Bible scholars—thrilled with new breakthroughs in Greek and Hebrew studies—would want to do the same. Maybe they sensed what now seems so clear: that the Middle Ages were over. And a golden age of Bible translation was at hand.

VI

GOSPEL
PREACHERS
OF THE
LATE
MIDDLE
AGES

CHAPTER TWELVE

John Wycliffe: Champion of Truth

A t what time all the world was in most desperate and vile estate, and the lamentable ignorance and darkness of God's truth had overshadowed the whole earth, this man stepped forth like a valiant champion." So wrote John Foxe, author of the sixteenth-century *Book of Martyrs*, a British chronicle glorifying the heroes of the Protestant Reformation. The man Foxe is speaking about was John Wycliffe, the first of these heroes in England. Born into a wealthy aristocratic family in North Yorkshire, Wycliffe spent most of his life at Oxford University—first as a student of arts and philosophy, then as a professor of theology, and finally as the most influential political and religious reformer of his time in England.

THE OXFORD YEARS

Wycliffe's early career was like that of many Oxford professors of his day. In the 1360s, he served as master of Balliol College and rector of one of the churches at the university. Later, he became master of Oxford's new Canterbury College. During his years at the university, Wycliffe wrote volumes of scholarly material, mostly in Latin. Generally, these writings were ambitious works on philosophy and religion. His doctoral lectures, for instance, were an impressive commentary on the whole Bible.

John Wycliffe

It was at Canterbury College that Wycliffe first tangled with church authorities. In 1367, the new archbishop—a monk named Simon Langham—removed Wycliffe and three of his students from Canterbury, replacing them with his fellow monks. This apparently made Wycliffe so angry that he sued the archbishop before the pope in Rome. And when the pope decided in favor of the monks, Wycliffe found it hard to forgive him.

Then, when King Edward III and his son John of Gaunt discovered Wycliffe's talents as a writer and disputant, they quickly drafted him to represent the Crown at the 1374 Bruges Conference with papal representatives. At the conference, which was called to settle various disputes between the Crown and the Roman Church, Wycliffe boldly argued that Rome had no right to tax the English clergy and make appointments within the English Church. He accused church officials of being obsessed with acquiring wealth and land. And he claimed that the king and the English lords had every right to appoint church officials and confiscate church lands.

But the pope ignored Wycliffe's arguments. Embittered, the reformer quickly became something of a professional advocate for the Crown and the nobility—against the pope and the Roman Church. He lambasted church authorities continually, until in 1377 the British archbishop summoned him to stand trial at St. Paul's Cross in London.

Oxford University, where Wycliffe taught for most of his life

But the powerful John of Gaunt came to Wycliffe's rescue, and the trial turned into a shouting match between Gaunt and the bishop of London. It ended in a riot.

As Wycliffe's writings became more political—targeted at forcing the pope to loosen his grip on the English Church—the pope countered with a number of bulls (edicts) calling Wycliffe "so deadly a pest" and ordering his immediate arrest. Finally, even the king commanded Wycliffe to be silent. But the feisty professor went right on preaching and writing. And his Oxford friends stood by him.

About this time, according to Foxe, Wycliffe became seriously ill, and several church friars came to offer him their advice. As Foxe (who was far from sympathetic toward Catholics in general) puts it, the friars "babbled much unto him touching the catholic church, the acknowledging of his errors, and the bishop of Rome [the pope]." Their chastisement, though, served only to rouse Wycliffe. Foxe relates that Wycliffe sat up in bed and retorted with these words from Scripture: "I shall not die, but I shall live, and declare the works of the Lord." And with that, he was healed.

Oxford University Chapel

The following year, Wycliffe's enemies summoned him before another church council—this time at Lambeth Palace in London. Once again, his influential supporters, including the king's mother (the Princess of Wales), came to his rescue. The trial was aborted.

Not long after this, a major schism developed between the Roman and French wings of the Catholic Church—so much so that the French cardinals elected a separate pope. This chaotic situation soured Wycliffe on church politics. From then on, his focus was entirely religious. He began to devote all his energies to helping the people of England understand the Bible. Before this, Wycliffe had been determined to reform the *Church*. Now, he was determined to reform—and to evangelize—the *people*. For the remaining years of his life, Wycliffe dedicated himself to preaching the gospel to his fellow countrymen and women—and to translating the Bible into their language.

THE "POOR PREACHERS"

Wycliffe and his closest followers began training a body of "poor preachers" to carry the gospel message throughout England. This ardent corps told the people about the Bible in a simple way that any-one—students, nobility, gentry, farmers, and common laborers alike—could understand. Drawn mostly from Wycliffe's university students, the preachers traveled on foot from village to village, wearing homely gowns made of light brown, unbleached wool.

If Wycliffe's preachers were unconventional, what they *taught* was nothing short of revolutionary. Like Wycliffe, they denied that the Roman Church had authority over other churches. They denied the authority of the pope. "The Pope of Rome," they said, "has no more in the keys of the Church than any other within the order of the priesthood." They denied, too, the validity of all traditions, cere-monies, and "observances" not specifically mentioned in Scripture. But the major theme of these zealous men—the theme that resounded with every sermon they preached—was the all-importance of the Holy Bible, the Word of God. "The Gospel is a rule sufficient of itself to rule the life of every Christian man here," they taught, "without any other rule."

THE "DEMOCRATISATION" OF SCRIPTURE

Wycliffe made his strongest statement about the supremacy of Scrip-ture over church doctrine in his Latin work *De Veritate Scripturae*, which he completed about 1378. In this tract, Wycliffe crushes, in the most scholarly of terms, what he sees as the medieval church teaching that "holy scripture is false." He refutes the time-honored doctrine of "medi-ate dominion"—the belief that people can learn Bible truth only through the medium of church hierarchy. Man's relationship with God is "immediate," Wycliffe contends. There are no barriers between *God* and His children, and consequently there should be no barriers between God's *Word* and His children.

The arguments in *De Veritate* add up to a conclusion that shook the fourteenth-century English social structure to its roots: the teaching that all God's children are, in a spiritual sense, equal. And that all God's children are equally able to understand *Scripture*.

In the minds of many, these ideas effectively wiped out the standing of both pope and Church since, for Wycliffe, the Bible was the only legitimate power governing humanity. "Holy Scripture is the preeminent authority for every Christian," he wrote, "and the rule of faith and of all human perfection." *Any* sincere Christian, he argued— not just priests—can preach the gospel. *Any* Christian can understand the Bible, or "Goddis Lawe." And *without* understanding the Bible, a Christian can't experience salvation!

Wycliffe felt that individuals should be responsible for their own spiritual welfare, a duty they can discharge only when they stay close to Christ. In the life of Christ, he believed, is the ultimate mes-sage of the Bible. For Wycliffe, Christ and Scripture were virtually synonymous, since—as he puts it—"Christ is the scripture we are bound to know." With an understanding of God's Word, the humblest Christian could be as fully empowered as the most exalted church official, Wycliffe felt. So it was crucial that every member of society— even people who couldn't read—be exposed to the Bible. Everyone should be included in the "democratisation" of Scripture.

THE PEASANTS' REVOLT

It's not too surprising that some of Wycliffe's followers used his teach-ings on Scriptural "democratisation" to justify political revolt, although the aristocratic reformer was horrified that this happened. In 1381, a man named Wat Tyler whipped the peasant classes in southern and eastern England into a full-scale uprising. The peasants were protest-ing attempts to lower their wages and a variety of other abuses con-nected with the feudal system. Eventually, they carried their rebellion into the streets of London, beheaded the Archbishop of Canterbury, and managed to extract some temporary concessions from Richard II. Their revolt crumbled when Tyler was killed in a scuffle with the mayor of London.

Because Tyler had been at one point an avid "Wycliffite," both Crown and Church blamed Wycliffe for the insurrection. Besides that, they were furious that Wycliffe dared to deny the central doctrine of the medieval Church—the doctrine of transubstantiation (the belief that the bread and the wine used in the sacrament of communion actually become the body and blood of Christ). Neither Church nor king could tolerate what they considered such blasphemy! So acting Oxford chancellor William De Berton asked a council of Catholic officials to condemn the reformer. The council was to the point. Wycliffe's doctrine could no longer be taught at Oxford—and the books he had written must be burned.

The following spring, Wycliffe faced another challenge. A council of bishops and theologians was called together to examine his record. They met at Blackfriars' Convent, just outside of London. A little after lunch on the first day of the conference, something astonishing happened. As Foxe describes the event, "A wonderful and terrible earthquake fell throughout all England." The conference participants were awestruck. Some suggested the earthquake was a divine omen indicating that the investigation should be stopped at once. But the archbishop refused to be unnerved. And in short order he persuaded the council to publish a thoroughgoing condemnation of all Wycliffe's "heresies."

THE FIRST WYCLIFFE BIBLE

In the wake of this "earthquake council" of 1382, Wycliffe had no choice but to retire to the small church at Lutterworth where he'd been rector for so many years. Yet, far from giving up on his mission, he was determined to lift it to a higher level—a universal level. He resolved to do something much more important than simply teach people about the Bible. He resolved to *give* them a Bible—the first complete version of Scripture ever published in the English language. As an initial step in this direction, he joined with a group of his followers who were already at work translating the Latin Vulgate into English.

No one knows exactly how involved Wycliffe himself was in translating what turned out to be the "Wycliffe Bible." At the very least, he inspired the project, which was carried out by his chief disciples, Nicholas Hereford and John Purvey. We do know that the translation proceeded in three phases, the first of which Hereford directed.

A longtime student and friend of Wycliffe, Hereford graduated from Oxford as a doctor of divinity in 1381. He was a popular campus preacher whose sermons stirred up a storm of resistance to the

Church. One of these sermons was so full of fury against the friars of St. Mary's that church authorities excommunicated him. Hereford escaped the death penalty only through the influence of John of Gaunt. In 1382, hoping for a reprieve, Hereford took his case to the pope at Rome. But this backfired. Instead of winning a reprieve, Hereford was condemned—and imprisoned for life. He managed to escape, though, in 1385.

Hereford had begun the Wycliffe Bible translation sometime before he left for his trial in Rome, possibly as early as 1378. He started with the Old Testament and proceeded as far as the apocryphal book of Baruch—stopping abruptly at the twentieth verse of chapter three. A note in the original manuscript reads simply, "Here endeth the translation of Nicholas Hereford." His excommunication and departure for Rome may explain why he halted work on the translation so suddenly.

Some five translators probably worked under Hereford, since scholars have noticed five distinct dialects within the manuscript. Yet there's a remarkable uniformity about the Hereford version, which—as a whole—is a word-for-word translation from the Latin Vulgate (Wycliffe didn't have access to the Hebrew and Greek texts). Hereford and his translators apparently revered the Vulgate so much that they didn't want to, or were afraid to, stray in the slightest from the holy wording they felt it contained. The result was an awkward and stilted brand of English, one that sounds far more Latinate than British.

After Hereford left for Rome, Wycliffe seems to have continued work on the translation—possibly alone—finishing the four Gospels and a good deal of the New Testament, and following the general style of Hereford's word-for-word translation.

WYCLIFFE'S EXPERIMENTAL TEXT

At the same time that Wycliffe was completing this conservative, literal translation of the Vulgate, he was privately pressing ahead with a radically new kind of Bible translation in a series of sermons he was writing. In these sermons, he quoted Scripture in a wonderfully fresh, homegrown, colloquial way. These Bible renderings have a powerful beauty about them—one that's more Anglo-Saxon than Latinate. And they're clearer and more concise than the involuted Vulgate text.

Wycliffe's purpose in these new renderings was to simplify Biblical ideas to make them understandable, especially to the uneducated laboring class he now wanted so passionately to reach. Even before his expulsion from Oxford, Wycliffe had begun to turn from a Latin-reading academic audience to the English-speaking public. More and more, he saw the public as the primary target for his message. Oxford had banished him; Richard and the aristocracy had deserted him. But the *common* people of England—and particularly the grass-roots gospel movement that Wycliffe's poor preachers had cultivated throughout the countryside—were wide open to the reformer's teachings. They were the audience he had to reach if he wanted his movement to continue. They were the ones who must learn to read the English Bible, to love it, to be guided by it, and to pass it along to their children. And they were the ones who would eventually preserve the Wycliffe Bible from extinction.

The Bible translations in Wycliffe's sermons are far removed from Hereford's slavish fidelity to the Vulgate. They're plain, vigorous,

Wycliffe's New Testament, 1848 edition

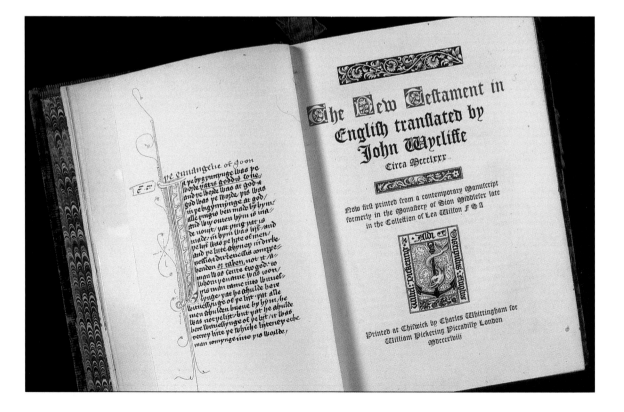

rhythmic, and spare—like Wycliffe's style of preaching. They're an obvious reaction against the ornate, scholarly sermonic style of the day.

Why didn't Wycliffe incorporate his lyrical experimental wordings into the complete Bible that later bore his name? Why did these gems remain buried in his sermons for future generations to find? Most likely, because church and state authorities of the early 1380s weren't ready for such a plainspoken and honest rendering of the Scriptures. And because Wycliffe and his followers knew that only the most conservative of texts, the most Vulgate-like, could win acceptance in a religious climate where it was considered blasphemous to give the Bible to the people at all.

THE FINAL WYCLIFFE BIBLE

After Wycliffe's passing in 1384, his followers—under the leadership of John Purvey, the reformer's secretary and closest associate—proceeded to revise the early Wycliffe Bible. (Purvey, an Oxford-educated minister, had been one of Wycliffe's "poor preachers.") Purvey knew how very readable and natural-sounding the translations in Wycliffe's sermons were. Nevertheless, he revised the original Wycliffe text in a conservative, relatively word-for-word way. He must have believed this was the way his mentor would have proceeded. Like Wycliffe, he had learned through years of persecution to be practical, to avoid offending the authorities more than was necessary.

Yet Purvey did offer a more idiomatic and natural-sounding text than had Hereford. And it was a better-researched text. As Purvey explains in his "General Prologue," he and his fellow revisers gave the original Wycliffe Bible at least four meticulous levels of review. They

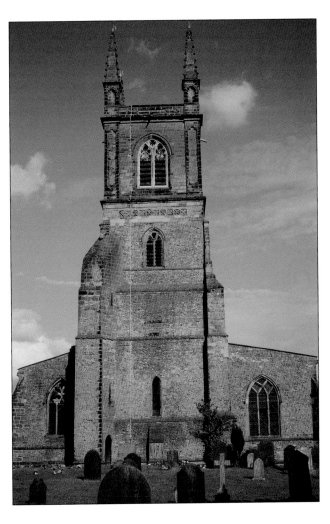

The church in Lutterworth where Wycliffe retired

compared it with "old Bibles," "old grammarians and old divines" (the writings of the Church Fathers), as well as a number of contemporary Bible commentaries. In addition, the revisers enlisted the help of "many good fellows . . . cunning at the correcting of the translation," who gave the Bible one last go-over for style and content.

Purvey's new Wycliffe Bible began circulating in manuscript form around 1388. Hungry to know more about the Bible, a book that had always been off limits for them, the British people took the new translation right to heart. Many of them learned to read just so they could labor through it on their own. Year by year, the number of Bible readers escalated dramatically. And the number of Wycliffe's followers increased too. Church authorities became alarmed. They branded these Wycliffites "Lollards," a negative term suggesting both laziness ("lolling" around) and the "muttering" of prayers. In desperation, the king ordered that the key Wycliffite supporters be seized. Both Hereford and Purvey were locked up in the Castle of Saltwood in Kent and tortured until they "recanted"–agreed to stop teaching Wycliffe's doctrines.

As it turned out, Hereford forsook Wycliffe's teachings forever. He even began *persecuting* the Lollards. This change of heart led him to a successful church career. He eventually became chancellor of St. Paul's Cathedral. And he finished his life as a Carthusian monk.

Purvey, on the other hand, remained true to the Wycliffite cause. During his long prison sentence, he continued to write Bible commentaries based on Wycliffe's lectures. In 1400, he was forced to recant again. As a reward for his submission, he was granted a position as vicar of West Hythe, in Kent. But he quietly clung to his Wycliffite beliefs and in a short time resigned his post. Purvey went on preaching the Lollard gospel throughout England, until he was imprisoned again in 1421. He apparently died an unrepentant Wycliffite.

Wycliffe's followers may have been persecuted and forced to give up their beliefs, but nothing could reverse the tide of public devotion to the Wycliffe Bible–not even Archbishop Arundel's 1408 prohibition of Bible reading. Frustrated by the people's determination to read the Scriptures in spite of this prohibition, Arundel wrote Pope

John XXII in 1412, blaming "that wretched and pestilent fellow John Wyckliffe" for this state of affairs. Out of sheer "malice," Arundel said, Wycliffe had "devised the expedient of a new translation of the scriptures into the mother tongue." And "the crown of the offence," the archbishop complained, was that "the translation were in a tongue comprehensible to all." To Arundel, this was unforgivable.

CHAPTER THIRTEEN

John Huss: Bohemian Advocate for Wycliffe

Two years before Wycliffe's passing in 1384, Richard II married Anne, the sister of Wenceslaus, king of Bohemia (now the Czech Republic). In England, the scholars and courtiers who accompanied Anne learned about Wycliffe's teachings. They carried his writings and ideals, especially his belief in the absolute supremacy of Scripture over church dogma, back to Bohemia. There, John Huss, a bright young student at the University of Prague, made Wycliffe's teachings his own and preached them with a fire that couldn't be quenched. Huss went on to become rector at Prague's Bethlehem Chapel, where he developed an enormously loyal following.

At first, the Bohemian archbishop tolerated Huss's activities. But the more ardently Huss preached Wycliffe's tenets, the more hostile the archbishop—and later the successive popes in Rome—became. In 1407, they ordered Huss to stop preaching. In 1409, they burned his books. And in 1412, they excommunicated him.

The Huss homestead

Throughout all this, Huss never stopped preaching. And the people of Prague filled his chapel, even when church authorities placed the city under a virtual siege. Finally, King Wenceslaus—determined to restore peace—forced Huss to leave Prague. Only then did the reformer stop preaching and turn to the pen as his key weapon against church abuses. He retired to the country, where he enjoyed the protection of his supporters in the nobility and composed his major theological book, *De Ecclesia*—a blazing defense of Wycliffe's doctrines.

It was this book, filled as it was with "heresy," that gave the Church all it needed to silence Huss for good. In *De Ecclesia*, he lifted large sections from Wycliffe's writings, translating them into Czech.

And like Wycliffe, Huss argued that the pope is not necessarily "the vicar of Jesus Christ." On the contrary, he said, a wicked pope is "the messenger of Antichrist." Huss also maintained that being excommunicated could be a good thing. "Every excommunication, by which a man is unjustly excommunicated," he said, "is unto him a blessing before God."

Huss's study

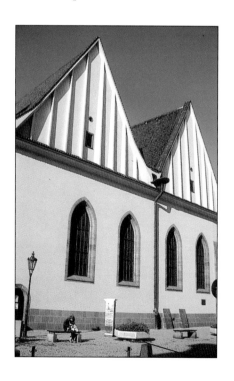

Bethlehem Chapel, Prague, where Huss preached

To church leaders, such statements were intolerable. So in 1414 a general church council being held at Constance, in Italy, demanded that Huss appear before them and defend himself against charges of heresy. Hoping to reverse the papal ban on his preaching and to gain some sort of approval for his Wycliffite beliefs, Huss traveled to Constance–trusting Holy Roman Emperor Sigismund's promise of safe conduct.

On his way through Germany, thousands of supporters turned out to greet Huss. "The streets were always full of people who were desirous to see and gratify him," writes Foxe. Once Huss arrived in Constance, though, it was clear that the emperor's "safe conduct" counted for nothing. Church authorities arrested him almost immediately and shuffled him from one prison to another. They kept him in chains, according to Foxe, or on a rack. Much of the time, he suffered from severe fever. When he was at last well enough to stand trial, he was brought before the council.

Huss answered the charges against him, one by one. But he refused to recant. He told the council that he would change his mind only if they could show him something in the Bible that proved he was wrong. But they couldn't. So, Foxe writes, "John Huss constantly answered as before, insomuch that they said he was obstinate and stubborn."

THE FINAL DAY

The next day, Huss was again summoned before the council. He begged them to let him speak one more time, but they refused. In despair, he cried out, "O Lord Jesu Christ! Whose Word is openly condemned here in this Council, unto Thee again I do appeal."

With that, according to Foxe, the judge pronounced the sentence against him: John Huss must die for being a "disciple of John Wickliff." And his books must be burned. The judge called Huss "a true and manifest heretic" and said that he must be "deposed and degraded" from his priestly status. Dropping to his knees, Huss cried out, "Lord Jesus Christ! forgive mine enemies, by whom thou knowest that I am falsely accused."

Foxe's graphic account says that the council mocked Huss and cursed him. They cut the skin off the crown of his head with shears and replaced it with a paper crown painted with three hideous-looking devils. One of the bishops said, "Now we commit thy soul unto the devil."

Huss was led to Prague's Gottlieben Gate—to be executed. There, he kneeled and repeated out loud the thirty-first and fifty-first Psalms. With deep spiritual joy in his face, he said, "Into thy hands, O lord! I commend my spirit." As the flames engulfed him, Huss sang aloud: "Jesu Christ! The Son of the living God! have mercy upon me." His ashes were thrown into the Rhine River.

Following Huss's execution, the Council of Constance turned its attention to eradicating the memory of John Wycliffe. They decreed that Wycliffe's body should be dug up from the grave in England where it had been buried some thirty years earlier. So Wycliffe's remains were exhumed, burned, and thrown into the river Swift. But, as Foxe concludes, "Though they digged up his body, burnt his bones, and drowned his ashes,

Statue of John Huss in Husinec, Bohemia, where he was born

The river Swift, where church officials threw Wycliffe's ashes

yet the Word of God and the truth of his doctrine, with the fruit and success thereof, they could not burn."

The ultimate significance of John Wycliffe's career lies way beyond the fact that he and his followers produced the first English Bible. What's most important is that his work won public acceptance for something that had always before been anathema: the concept of Bible translation for the common people. In this sense, Wycliffe's career—and later Huss's—planted the seeds of the vernacular gospel in England, Bohemia, and Germany.

This is not to say that there had been no vernacular Scriptures in Europe and England before Wycliffe's time. There had. As we've said earlier, fragments of Scripture—and possibly the whole Bible—had been translated into French, Italian, and German. But common folk had never seen these Bible texts. The Scriptures had circulated only among aristocrats and monks and a few church officials. They were written *by* the elite, *for* the elite.

Wycliffe's lifework changed all this. He and his followers put out a Bible that was not just for the elite. It was a Bible designed to be *published*. It was directed to the hearts of simple people, even though its language was formal and stilted. And more than that, Wycliffe supported the Bible's publication with a philosophy of vernacular Bible translation—one that he had developed over the years. His scholarly works and his long teaching career at Oxford had conveyed to a whole generation of church leaders the conviction that anyone—regardless of sex, status, age, education, or profession—could understand the Bible.

Wycliffe's disciples and the poor preachers, in turn, communicated this Scriptural philosophy to the people. So by the time the public actually received the Wycliffe Bible, they were ready to embrace it without reservation. They were already convinced that they should have the Bible. And they knew in advance that they had the God-given capacity to *understand* it—even though they might have to learn how to read first!

When the Church prohibited Bible reading in 1408, the tide of popular devotion to Wycliffe's text was irreversible. After Archbishop Arundel's interdict, people went right on reading Wycliffe's Bible—even though they had to smuggle its precious chapters from hand to hand, farmhouse to farmhouse, village to village.

Despite edicts and bulls and executions, British citizens continued for more than a century to read tattered fragments of Wycliffe's Bible. And the Hussites (the Wycliffites of Bohemia) pressed on all the more committedly in their quest for Bible truth after John Huss's martyrdom. It was they who helped water the seeds of the gospel in Germany—seeds Huss had helped to sow on his way to the fateful Council of Constance.

Before the end of the century, there emerged in Germany another great Wycliffite reformer, the man who fathered the Protestant Reformation. It was this man, Martin Luther, who produced the first Bible written *entirely in ordinary spoken language.* And the "Luther Bible" was to set the standard for the great Bibles of the Reformation.

VII
THE
REVOLUTION
THAT
RETURNED
THE BIBLE TO
THE PEOPLE

CHAPTER FOURTEEN

Martin Luther Launches the Protestant Reformation

"The Bible is alive, it speaks to me; it has feet, it runs after me; it has hands, it lays hold of me." So wrote Martin Luther, the great reformer who fought to give the Bible to the German people.

In translating the Bible for his fellow Germans, Luther opened floodgates of thought in Western Europe that could never again be shut. His Bible—the Luther Bible—set the standard for future translations of the Scriptures from Latin and Hebrew and Greek into languages ordinary people could understand—such as French, Spanish, Portuguese, Dutch, Swedish, Danish, Icelandic, and English.

Luther's bold break from the Roman Catholic Church changed the face of Western Christendom forever. This, in turn, created a climate in which men, women, and children could finally own and read the Bible without fear of reprisal.

LUTHER'S EARLY LIFE

Luther was born in 1483 in the small town of Eisleben, Germany, not far from the Thuringian Forest. Shortly after his birth, the family moved to the nearby town of Mansfeld, where his father, Johann Luther, worked in the copper mines. Although the family was poor, Luther's father worked hard to give him, as well as his seven brothers and sisters, a good upbringing. Johann was especially ambitious for young Martin and dreamed that someday his son would become a wealthy lawyer.

At a time when very few in the peasant class were educated, Johann gave his son excellent schooling. When the young Luther was seven, he began school in Mansfeld, where he learned Latin, the language of the Church, and the law. After finishing his early education, Luther went on to the University of Erfurt, where he studied language, logic, and philosophy. It was at the university library that he first saw a complete Bible, undoubtedly in Latin. Fascinated, Luther spent endless hours reading it. He went on to complete his master of arts degree in early 1505 and, at his father's urging, entered law school at Erfurt.

In July of that year, however, an incident took place that changed the course of his life. As the story goes, Luther was walking back to Erfurt after a visit with his family when a lightning bolt almost hit him. Terrified, he vowed to join a religious order if God would save him. Within two weeks, in spite of his father's protest, he left law school and joined the Augustinian order of monks in Erfurt. He was twenty-two years old.

LUTHER THE MONK

Luther embraced the stern, disciplined life of a monk enthusiastically. He shaved the crown of his head and put on a friar's black cowl and hood. He lived in an unheated, six-by-nine-foot cell and ate his meals in silence. Within a year, he took his final vows of poverty, chastity, and obedience. In February 1507 he was ordained a priest.

So diligent was Luther about his vocation that the vicar general of the Augustinians, Johann von Staupitz, early singled him out for a teaching position at the newly founded University of Wittenberg, where Staupitz was professor of theology. There, Luther earned his doctorate in theology in 1512 and was selected to succeed Staupitz when the professor retired.

In 1516, the great Dutch scholar Erasmus published his highly accurate edition of the Greek New Testament. Luther quickly learned Greek so he could get to the literal meaning of the Gospels.

About this time, Luther became deeply disturbed. "Day by day," he wrote, "I become worse and more wretched." He was tormented by the belief that he was an unforgiven sinner who didn't know how to find God. Besides that, he became increasingly disillusioned with the Church, as he began to realize how far it had wandered from its early roots.

It was Luther's love of Scripture, however, that delivered him from his misery. Suddenly one day, he was struck by this statement of the Apostle Paul: "The just shall live by faith" (Rom. 1:17). All at once, Luther understood that God justifies Christians on the basis of the purity of their faith. From that time forward, Luther had an entirely new view of the Bible. Later he wrote, "The whole of the Scriptures took on a new meaning, and it became to me inexpressibly sweet in greater love, so that the passage of Paul became to me a gate of heaven."

LUTHER CONDEMNS THE CHURCH

Once Luther understood that salvation depends upon the strength of a person's own faith, he became convinced that the "works" and rituals required by the medieval Church were no longer essential to achieve unity with God. He became particularly concerned over the Church's recent practice of selling "indulgences," or forgiveness for sins.

Luther drew up a list of ninety-five theses, or reasons, why the selling of indulgences was wrong. According to tradition, he nailed the list on the door of the castle church, the Schlosskirche, at Wittenberg, in October 1517, openly challenging anyone to debate him on the issue. Within days, his "Ninety-five Theses"—printed quickly on the newly invented printing presses in Germany—had swept over the country. The German people rallied passionately to Luther's support.

In 1519, the theologian and professor Johann Eck challenged Luther to a theological debate that lasted ten days. Eck cornered Luther into denouncing the authority of both the pope and the Church

Luther fixing his theses to the door of the Schlosskirche at Wittenberg, a painting by Hugo Vogel

councils—and into asserting that the Bible is the only authority Christians should accept. This statement clearly branded Luther as a heretic in the eyes of the papacy, since John Huss had burned at the stake a hundred years earlier for refusing to recant the same beliefs.

Luther spent the next year writing books to refute the arguments of his adversaries. One of the ideas he advanced in these books was what he called "the priesthood of believers"—the concept that all Christians are on equal footing in the eyes of God. Therefore, he concluded, no special priesthood is required to mediate between God and humanity.

The more Luther wrote, the bolder and more plainspoken he became. In June of 1520, the pope condemned all of Luther's publications.

THE DIET OF WORMS

In January of 1521, the pope excommunicated Luther. That same month, Holy Roman Emperor Charles V called a meeting of the German princes—since referred to as the Diet of Worms—to decide what to do with him. After a hot debate, the diet decided to summon Luther to appear before them and to ask him to repudiate his views. He requested one day to consider his response.

The next evening, when the authorities brought Luther into the packed hall, he reportedly said, "I cannot and I will not recant anything, for to go against conscience is neither right nor safe. God help me. Amen."

Sympathetic members of the diet tried to convince Luther to compromise, but he refused. Within a month, Emperor Charles pronounced the Edict of Worms, which declared Luther an outlaw and forbade anyone to help him or read his books. But Luther's friend the elector of Saxony came to his rescue, hiding him safely in the castle at Wartburg.

TRANSLATING THE NEW TESTAMENT

Despite deep mental darkness, Luther translated Erasmus' Greek New Testament into German. He finished the translation in just eleven

weeks. The completed New Testament was published in
September of 1522. It was a handsome volume, with
woodcuts by Lucas Cranach and reproductions from
Albrecht Dürer's paintings on the Apocalypse. The
German public bought approximately five thousand
copies of the Testament in the first two months. And
they *read* Luther's Testament, the Edict of Worms
notwithstanding.

Luther's Bible in German,
1729 edition

The arrangement of books in Luther's Testament
was new—and entirely his own. He ordered the books
according to their emphasis on Christ Jesus. Nearly every
Bible translated since Luther's time kept his New Testament
order. Luther's New Testament shunned many of the corrupted
Vulgate translations of words—words emphasizing the Roman Catholic
liturgy. Instead of the word *priest,* for example, Luther used *Saviour* or
elder. Instead of *church,* he used *congregation.* And instead of *do penance,*
he used *repent.*

THE PEASANTS' REVOLT

Meanwhile, momentum was building among Luther's more radical
followers toward open violence against the abuses of the Church and
the wealthy aristocrats. The longer Luther remained in hiding, the
greater the danger that radicals would take over his movement. Hotheads like Andreas Karlstadt encouraged Luther's followers to raid
church services—smashing images and roughing up the priests. This
alarmed Luther and his closest friend, the ever-gentle scholar Philipp
Melanchthon, Protestant reformer and fellow professor at the University of Wittenberg.

Yet Luther felt pressured by the liberals to make a public statement that monks and nuns should be out in the world preaching the
gospel rather than leading cloistered lives. He even ended up approv-
ing marriage for former monks and nuns, although he said, "They will
never thrust a wife on me!"

By the spring of 1522, when zealots from Zwickau began urging
the people of Wittenberg to abandon the Bible, Luther couldn't stand it

Martin Luther's family: father, Johann; mother, Margaretha; Martin; wife, Catherine; and daughter, Magdalena

any longer. Forgetting about his personal safety, he rode back to Wittenberg and took firm hold of his followers. In cogently worded sermons, he called on the people to renounce violence and maintain the unity of their movement.

Gradually, Luther reformed the order of church service in Wittenberg—introducing one that featured Bible reading and preaching in the German language. And he added another distinctive element: beautiful German hymns, a number of which he composed himself. But for some, especially the peasants oppressed by the land-owner class, these reforms weren't enough. They called Luther names like "Dr. Liar" because he discouraged violence. And, by 1525, a full revolution was in motion.

At first, Luther sympathized with the rebels, but when he saw landowners being killed and castles being burned, he did his best to call a halt to the uprisings. He traveled around the countryside, preaching against bloodshed and telling the peasants not to politicize his message. His demand was for *spiritual*, not political, freedom. "If the peasant is in open rebellion," he said, "then he is outside the law of God, for rebellion is not simply murder, but it is like a great fire which attacks and lays waste a whole land." Some people never understood—and never forgave—Luther for supporting the landowners and government authorities at this time. To him, though, it was the only way to save his cause.

MARRIAGE AND FAMILY

Four years after Luther declared he'd never marry, Catherine von Bora—a nun who had been inspired by Luther's writings to renounce her vows—proposed to him. She'd been sent to a convent against her will by her father and had never adapted to monastic life. She escaped, though, along with eleven other nuns, with one of Luther's followers, who hid the women between barrels of herring in his delivery wagon and brought them to Wittenberg.

Some of the women returned to their families; others married. Only Catherine remained to be placed, and she suggested that she marry Luther, feeling he needed a wife to care for him. At first he thought she was joking, but he soon came to believe the marriage was part of God's plan. At the very least, it saved her from the life of poverty and homelessness that an unattached ex-nun might have suffered at that time.

The two became deeply devoted to each other and had six children. They wanted above all to set a standard in their home for good Christian living. A year after the marriage, Luther wrote, "My Katie is in all things so obliging and pleasing to me that I would not exchange my poverty for the riches of Croesus." Their home was a haven for victims of the upheavals of the Reformation—people fleeing persecution as well as former monks and nuns who needed temporary shelter.

Because Luther refused the profits from his books and spent so much money helping the poor and needy, the Luthers had to live simply. But when they were low on funds, Luther would say, "Kate, God is rich. He will give us some more."

TRANSLATION OF THE
OLD TESTAMENT

After his marriage, Luther completed his translation of the Old Testament, working with a committee of scholarly luminaries and close friends—including Melanchthon. He nicknamed the group Sanhedrin, the name for the ancient governing body of the Jews. Luther took the lead in the work and developed the theory of translation the group

A 1708 edition of Luther's Old and New Testaments

used. Primarily, he believed that the Old Testament words should sound right in German. So the group had to strike a balance between what sounded good to the ear and what was correct in a literal sense. This meant the Sanhedrin couldn't rush the work. Sometimes they labored for days over just a few lines of Scripture.

Luther didn't want his Bible or the characters in it to sound Hebraic or foreign; he wanted them to sound

Statue of Martin Luther on the Reformation monument in Worms, Germany

thoroughly German. "We are now sweating over a German translation of the Prophets," he wrote. "O God, what a hard and difficult task it is to force these writers, quite against their wills, to speak German." And he wanted the German to be good, clear, "marketplace" language. To accomplish this, Luther and his translators used courtly language as their base but mixed it in with the German dialects. The effect was wording that was easy to read and beautiful to listen to.

When Luther and his committee finally completed their monumental translation in 1534, they made it available at a price nearly everyone could afford. Therefore, the Bible's majestic poetry and healing message reached Germans almost universally. No other book in the German language has matched its popularity. Its sonorous lines entered the hearts and minds of all the people, never to disappear, and it set the standard for the German language.

LUTHER'S HERITAGE

The personal difficulties Luther endured were staggering. Nearly all his life, he struggled with ill health. But he never stopped working. He counted on his faith and prayers to carry him through. And, of course, there was the relentless opposition to his work. When his death in 1546 was announced at the Council of Trent—the Roman Catholic council called to respond to the Protestant challenge—the council members sent up a cheer.

Yet Luther's accomplishments were far more significant than the opposition he encountered. Primarily, he gave the Bible to the German people. But he had a great deal to do with giving the Scriptures to *all* of us. Nearly every later Bible translator, of whatever nationality, used Luther's text as a key model. The war he waged against Bible illiteracy, church and state authorities who wanted to suppress Scripture reading, and those who sought to politicize his ministry reestablished the Bible as the core of the Christian way of life.

CHAPTER FIFTEEN

William Tyndale's Translation: Cornerstone of the English Bible

It all started around 1515, according to tradition, at the White Horse Inn near Cambridge University, in England. A group of young college lecturers in theology and Bible studies met there regularly to talk about Luther's "heretical" ideas. From this group would come some of the outstanding leaders of the Protestant movement in England—men like Bible translator Miles Coverdale and future Archbishop of Canterbury Thomas Cranmer. But no figure in this group would make a more indelible mark on the future of the English Church than an earnest young student of Scripture named William Tyndale.

A native of Gloucestershire, Tyndale had taken his master's degree at Oxford, where he'd studied Greek. At that time, he'd developed his lifelong love of the Bible. Around 1515, he had left Oxford to study Greek at Cambridge under the famous scholar Erasmus. There the radicals at the White Horse Inn apparently fired him with a passion to give the Word of God to everybody in England—not just a privileged few. As he later promised his adversaries, "If God spare my life, ere many years I will cause a boy that driveth a plough shall know more of the Scriptures than thou doest."

MOVING FORWARD FROM WYCLIFFE'S BIBLE

Of course, John Wycliffe had translated the Bible into English more than a hundred years earlier. But Wycliffe hadn't known Hebrew and Greek. So, as we've said earlier, his Bible was simply an English translation of the defective Latin Vulgate. Besides that, in 1408 the church authorities had forbidden people to read it, "upon pain of greater ex-communication."

Yet Tyndale knew that the common folk of England were hungry for a *complete* Bible in their own language—a Bible they could easily afford and keep in their homes. He also knew that the marvelous new printing presses developed in Europe had made this a real possibility. Johannes Gutenberg had printed the first complete

Tyndale translating the Bible, a painting by W. Johnstone

Bible—an edition of the Vulgate—in Germany in 1455. And William Caxton had brought the printing process to England in 1470.

The time was right for an English Bible in other ways too. In 1453, when Constantinople, capital of the Greek Christian Empire, fell to the Turkish Muslim conquerors, the eminent Bible scholars of the East had fled to Europe. And they'd brought with them their understanding of the original Greek and Hebrew Scriptural texts.

These Greek scholars stirred up a whirlwind of Biblical studies on the Continent and in England. Erasmus, for instance, put out his revolutionary edition of the Greek New Testament in 1516, while Tyndale was studying under him at Cambridge. During this period, too, printed editions of Scripture started appearing in various vernacular languages throughout Europe—in Danish, Dutch, Slavic, Bohemian, Russian, Italian, French, and Spanish.

TYNDALE'S NEW TESTAMENT

Around 1520, Tyndale became so frustrated by the conservatism of the clergy that he was totally convinced of the need for church reform. A new version of Scriptures, he felt, could expose the corruption of the clergy and show people how far the Church had wandered from Bible truth. So Tyndale went to London, hoping that Bishop Cuthbert Tunstall would help him realize his dream of producing an English Bible.

Tunstall, a church hard-liner, gave him a cold reception. But a wealthy London cloth merchant named Humphrey Monmouth let Tyndale stay in his home for six months while he began translating the New Testament from Erasmus' Greek text and Luther's German Bible.

Tyndale lived like a hermit, working day and night. Eventually, though, he began to feel that the atmosphere in England was too hostile for him. So in 1524 he went to the free city of Hamburg, Germany. And he almost surely spent time with Martin Luther in Wittenberg.

SMUGGLING THE NEW TESTAMENTS
INTO ENGLAND

Once he'd finished his New Testament, certainly by 1526, Tyndale secretly printed two editions of it in Worms and smuggled them into England in bales of cloth.

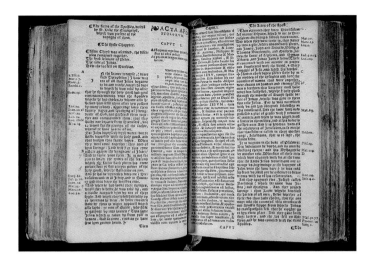

A fourth edition of Tyndale's New Testament, 1550

In England, Tyndale's New Testament caused a furor. The people loved it and bought up the text by the thousands. But church authorities were incensed. Bishop Tunstall said the translation had two thousand errors in it. He especially objected to its antiecclesiastical slant, noting that Tyndale translated the word *church* as *congregation,* and *priest* as *elder.* Also, he detested Tyndale's introductions and marginal glosses, most of which criticized the pope and the Roman Church.

Bishop Tunstall decreed that all Tyndale's New Testaments be destroyed. And King Henry VIII said that the translation was "onely fayned to enfecte the peopull." Agitated church authorities held massive book burnings in London, Oxford, and Antwerp. The campaign to eradicate Tyndale's Bible was so successful that, of the eighteen thousand copies printed between 1525 and 1528, only two fragmented copies remain today.

Tyndale's Testament, in the short time it circulated in England, won a permanent place with the people. Its wordings were fresh and lyrical, conveying the pure meaning of Scripture as never before in English. Their simplicity went straight to the heart.

Continuing his work, Tyndale moved from one European city to another to avoid capture by church authorities. At one point, he was shipwrecked on the Dutch coast and lost his translation of Deuteronomy. But he continued on to Antwerp, where he retranslated Deuteronomy and finished translating the Pentateuch and the book of Jonah.

In Antwerp, Tyndale met a man named Henry Phillips, who professed to be an ardent supporter of the Reformation. Actually, Phillips was a devout Roman Catholic. He betrayed Tyndale directly into the hands of the imperial authorities, who slapped him into prison in Vilvorde Castle, near Brussels. Tradition has it that, even in prison, Tyndale pressed forward with his work. During that time, he may have completed a manuscript translation of Joshua, Judges, Ruth, Samuel, Kings, and Chronicles.

A year later, in 1536, Tyndale was tried for heresy and condemned to death. Henry VIII, who'd always thought of Tyndale as an enemy, did nothing to help the reformer. So Tyndale's execution was inevitable. He was strangled and then burned at the stake. His last words were "Lord, open the King of England's eyes."

At the very moment that Tyndale uttered those words, the king's eyes *were*, in fact, being opened to the value of publishing–and even putting his royal stamp of approval on–Tyndale's Bible. Thomas Cranmer, Tyndale's friend from Cambridge days, had recently become Archbishop of Canterbury. And, along with Thomas Cromwell, the king's chief adviser, Cranmer had taken up the cause for Tyndale's English Bible.

Cranmer had always loved the Scriptures. At Cambridge, he'd spent three whole years immersed in Bible study and required all of his students there to be experts in Scripture. In 1534, two years before Tyndale's death, Cranmer and his bishops petitioned the king for a new translation of the Bible to be made available to all the people. But what Cranmer really wanted was the king to sponsor *Tyndale's* Bible.

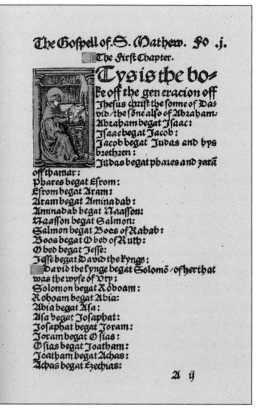

Page from an 1862 facsimile of Tyndale's Bible

THE COVERDALE BIBLE

In the meantime, the king did allow another English translation of the Bible to be made available to the public. This was one by Tyndale's friend from the White Horse Inn group, Miles Coverdale.

For years, Coverdale had corresponded with Cromwell about Bible study and translation. And he may even have worked briefly with Tyndale in Hamburg on the translation of the Pentateuch. Although Coverdale's knowledge of Greek and Hebrew was limited, he did know Latin and German. And he had a marvelous command of the English language. His Bible is based primarily on the Latin Vulgate, Luther's German Bible, and Tyndale's translation.

At that time, Henry was faced with enormous public pressure for a Bible to replace Tyndale's New Testament, which he and the bishops had snatched off the market out of fear that it might cause a revolution in both Church and state. Cromwell saw in Coverdale's Bible an opportunity to meet this public demand, so he persuaded the king to support Coverdale's work. In 1535, while Tyndale was still imprisoned on the Continent, Coverdale's Bible was printed and released in England—the first *complete* Bible to be published in English. Coverdale dedicated it to King Henry.

Few were satisfied with Coverdale's Bible. At best it was a watered-down version of Tyndale's Bible, with the radicalism removed. It represented merely a translation and revision of *other* Bible translations, not a reworking from the original Greek and Hebrew texts. Its redeeming qualities were its clarity and readability. But neither Cromwell and Cranmer nor the English populace was ready to give up on having Tyndale's complete translation back in print.

Title page from 1537 edition of Matthew's Bible

THE MATTHEW'S BIBLE

A close friend of Tyndale, John Rogers, devised a scheme to republish the reformer's New Testament. Rogers had first met Tyndale in 1534 in Antwerp, where Rogers was a Catholic chaplain to the English merchants. Tyndale quickly made a Protestant out of him. After Tyndale was imprisoned, he entrusted Rogers with all his materials, including his nearly completed translation of the Old Testament.

The year Tyndale was executed, Rogers began compiling a complete Bible based on Tyndale's unfinished manuscript. He used Coverdale's text to fill in the gaps. Rogers added prefaces and marginal notes to the new Bible—all of which were strongly anti-Catholic in tone. Rogers was careful, though, to avoid Tyndale's fate. He published his Bible under the pseudonym Thomas Matthew—possibly the name of one of his financial backers. And, hoping for royal approval, he dedicated the work to King Henry and his current wife, Lady Jane.

Rogers printed fifteen hundred of these Bibles in Antwerp and sent an advance copy to Cranmer in England. The archbishop immediately told Cromwell, "I like it [the Bible] better than any other translation heretofore made." And he urged Cromwell to get the king to license it right away. Within a week, Cromwell persuaded the king—who apparently never suspected that the "Matthew's Bible" was a disguised Tyndale text—to allow the Bible to be sold throughout England. In 1537, therefore, only one year after Tyndale was martyred, his Bible was republished and distributed in his native land.

Initials of John Rogers in the Matthew's Bible of 1537 (the only indication of the translator's true identity)

THE GREAT BIBLE

The Matthew's Bible, though, had built-in problems. Its prefaces and notes were so strongly controversial that the king and the conserva-

Illustration of medieval-styled gatherers of manna, as Moses looks on, from the Great Bible of 1539

tives in the English Church ended up taking offense at them. So Cromwell soon knew he had to devise a substitute Bible. And he turned to Coverdale, who was known as a skillful compromiser and editor, to come up with a new English text for the king to approve.

Although this new Bible would later be advertised on its title page as an original translation from the Greek and Hebrew, Coverdale provided nothing of the kind. He, and perhaps some other scholars of his choosing, merely edited Tyndale's text—melding it with his own earlier text and that of the Matthew's Bible, leaving out all the controversial notes and prefaces

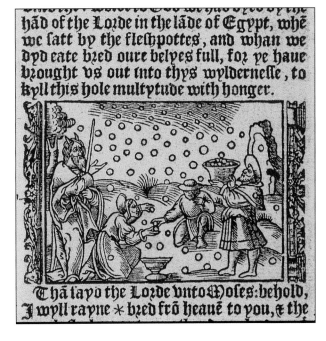

written by Rogers. This quick editorial process completed, Coverdale and a wealthy grocer named Edward Whitchurch went to Paris to print the Bible.

There were complications in Paris, however. Catholic authorities halted the work and confiscated the printing sheets. Somehow, Coverdale and Whitchurch were able to rescue enough of their materials—presses, printing sheets, types, and even workmen—to complete the printing process in London. The result was a magnificent large edition, nicknamed the Great Bible because of its size.

Because Rogers's contentious notes had been removed from the Great Bible, Henry at once agreed to put the stamp of "royal authority" on it. And Cromwell issued orders for every parish in the land to have a copy of the Bible "sett up summe convenyent place within the churche," so that all the parishioners could read it.

THE CRANMER BIBLE

In April of 1540, Cromwell sponsored a second edition of the Great Bible, this one with a preface by Cranmer as archbishop. Cranmer's statement stands as one of the most passionate endorsements of Scripture reading in the history of the English Bible. He writes, "In the scriptures be the fat pastures of the soul. . . . Here maee all manner of persons, men, women, young, old, learned, unlearned, rich, poor, priests, laymen, lords, ladies, officers, tenants, and mean men, virgins, wives, widows, lawyers, merchants, artificers, husbandmen, and all manner of persons of what estate or condition soever they be, may in this book learn all things what they should not do, as well concerning Almighty God, as also concerning themselves and all other." The archbishop went on to say, "Briefly, to the reading of the scripture none can be enemy . . . [unless] they know not scripture to be the most healthful medicine." This edition became known as the Cranmer Bible.

Two months after the publication of this Bible, Cromwell—chief architect of the plan to publish Tyndale's Bible—was thrown into the Tower of London. His conservative enemies had at last orchestrated his downfall, and in July of 1540 this leader of the Protestant Reformation in England was beheaded.

Back cover of a fourth edition of Tyndale's Bible, 1550

After Cromwell's demise, the Church took a more conservative turn. Henry issued an injunction that prevented people from discussing the Bible in public. In 1547, Henry's young son, Edward, a zealous Protestant, took the throne of England. With his support, Cranmer led the Church in a more radical direction and turned out the beautiful Book of Common Prayer, the service book for the Anglican Church. In this book, Cranmer featured a number of psalms and other Scriptural passages to be used in the worship services. So, the people could daily, for the very first time in England, hear the Word of God read or sung aloud in church. But all this soon came to an end. Edward's reign was cut off by his early death, and his Catholic sister, Queen Mary, came to the throne.

QUEEN MARY BANS BIBLE READING

During her five-year reign, Mary dedicated herself single-mindedly to restoring Catholicism in England. She and her Spanish husband, Philip II, executed hundreds of Protestants who wanted to maintain their faith and continue reading their Bibles. John Rogers was the first martyr to burn at the stake. Cranmer burned in 1556. Countless others—including Coverdale—fled to the Continent and joined the Protestant colony of exiles at Geneva.

Most of the original White Horse Inn group were lost during Mary's brief but harrowing reign. Yet their legacy, the Tyndale Bible, still lives in the hearts and minds of English-speaking people everywhere. For it is Tyndale's voice that sings longest and strongest and most ineffably in the lines of the King James Bible.

CHAPTER SIXTEEN

The Geneva Bible: A Gift from the English Exiles

For centuries the city of Geneva, perched high in the Alps on the border between France and Switzerland, was a haven for political and religious refugees. To this idyllic lakeside setting, religious exiles from continental Europe and England fled by the thousands in the mid-1500s to escape persecution and map out the future of the Protestant Reformation. It was here that a colony of English Protestant refugees found a sanctuary where they could translate and publish a new version of the Scriptures for the people of their homeland—a version that came to be known as the Geneva Bible.

ZWINGLI: FIRST LEADER OF THE SWISS REFORMATION

Paralleling Martin Luther's Reformation work in Germany was the Protestant movement in the small, independent city-states of Switzerland. The push for reform started in the German-speaking city of Zurich, under the leadership of Ulrich Zwingli.

Zwingli was born in the mountains of eastern Switzerland. He was ordained a Catholic priest in 1506. During his first pastorship, though, he came under the influence of the Dutch reformer Erasmus. This inspired him to learn Greek and Hebrew, as well as to devote himself to Scriptural study. Armed with this knowledge and fired with resentment against the abuses of the Church, he delivered, in 1519, a series of sermons that launched the Protestant Reformation in Switzerland.

That same year, Zwingli had a healing experience that changed his thinking forever. He recovered from the plague that had swept over Zurich. For the first time, he felt the presence of God. From then on, he was ready to fight for the reformers' cause, hailing Luther as a "new Elias."

Zwingli became the acknowledged leader of the Swiss Reformation. His movement took root in city after city, in spite of opposition from the Church. And he died defending Zurich against an invasion by Catholic troops in 1531.

FRENCH REFUGEES IN GENEVA

The following year a young French Protestant named Guillaume Farel fled to Geneva from Paris, where the authorities had just cracked down on followers of the "new religion." The citizens of Geneva loved the radical ideas of this fiery preacher. By 1536 he'd persuaded them to accept the Protestant faith as their official religion.

Farel convinced another young Protestant from Paris, John Calvin, to settle in Geneva. Calvin had been trained in both the priesthood and the law at the University of Paris, where he'd first heard about the Protestant faith. His conversion experience reversed the direction of his life and convinced him that his mission was to return Christianity to its apostolic purity.

When Calvin came to Geneva in 1536, he'd just published the first edition of his one great book on theology, *Institutes of the Christian Religion*. Over a twenty-two-year period, he expanded this book, until it eventually became almost a guidebook for the Protestant Reformation.

Calvin urged the absolute supremacy of God, explaining that the emphasis on saints and the Virgin Mary in the medieval Church had led Christianity away from worshiping the one God. Like Luther, he believed that a person's faith alone justifies him or her in the eyes of God. But he carried this point even further, arguing that people are "predestined" to either eternal life or eternal damnation. And Calvin felt that worship services should be as simple as possible, based strictly on Scripture.

Calvin ruled the Geneva church firmly, but he showed deepest compassion toward the five thousand religious refugees who flooded the city between 1549 and 1559. He nurtured them spiritually, encouraging them to take the model of his church-state community back to their homelands. For him, the presence of so many refugees in Geneva offered an irresistible opportunity to create a kind of missionary army of Bible readers. And he persuaded the Frenchman Theodore Beza, the finest Bible scholar of the Reformation, to come teach them.

ARRIVAL OF ENGLISH REFUGEES
IN GENEVA

When the Catholic Queen Mary (Bloody Mary, as she was nicknamed) came to the throne in England in 1553, she launched—as mentioned previously—a reign of terror to rid her realm of Protestants. So, to escape almost certain execution, the leaders of the new religion took advantage of Calvin's hospitality in Geneva—staying there until Mary's death in 1558.

Among these Englishmen were some of the outstanding Bible scholars of the age. According to most accounts, it was William Whittingham and John Knox, both hard-core Calvinists, who first became interested in starting a new Bible translation, shortly after their arrival in Geneva in 1555. The two had met in Frankfurt, where Knox was preacher to the English exiles. But when Whittingham and Knox were expelled from Frankfurt for their radicalism, they went straight to Geneva, where they knew they'd be welcome.

Map of the Exodus and subsequent events from the Geneva Bible, 1560

Knox had converted to Protestantism in the mid-1540s and quickly became the champion of the Reformation movement in Scotland, his homeland. A scintillating evangelical preacher, he was one of the last Protestant leaders to take flight after Mary became queen.

As soon as Knox arrived in Geneva, Calvin tapped him to preach to the English exiles. Knox loved Geneva and called the church there "the most perfect school of Christ" since early Christianity.

WHITTINGHAM'S NEW TESTAMENT

Geneva was, at this time, alive with the thrill of Bible scholarship. When the English exiles arrived, the French exiles were already laboring over a new Bible translation to send home. And Calvin's friend Theodore Beza, whom he'd known since the days when the two of them converted to the Protestant faith in France, was putting the last touches on his Latin translation of the Greek New Testament.

Inspired by all this and encouraged by Calvin, Whittingham and some other English Bible scholars began a revision of the Great Bible's New Testament. They based their work on the best Bible scholarship Geneva had to offer, including Calvin's New Testament *Commentaries* and Beza's new Latin Bible.

When Whittingham and his friends finished their New Testament in 1557, it was the best English translation yet. Calvin himself wrote an enthusiastic introduction for it. In addition to its unprecedented accuracy, the New Testament included verse divisions for the first time in an English Bible. Whittingham had gotten the idea for verse divisions from the printer Robert Estienne, one of the French refugees in Geneva. Whittingham also supplied marginal notes for his New Testament. And he italicized words he'd added to the text, words that weren't in the original Greek and Hebrew.

Back home in England, Whittingham's New Testament was received with celebration, even though it had to be distributed through an underground network. The tremendous reception the people gave the new text encouraged Whittingham to launch a new translation—this time of the *entire* Bible. So he gathered together a team of English Bible scholars living in Switzerland and began the work immediately. They named the new version of Scripture they produced the Geneva Bible.

TRANSLATORS OF THE GENEVA BIBLE

The exact makeup of the translation team seems to have been kept secret, maybe to protect the participants. But we do know who some of them were. In addition to Whittingham, who acted as supervisor, John Knox and Miles Coverdale almost surely contributed. Coverdale had, of course, produced the first complete English Bible in 1535. Both Knox and Coverdale would have brought marvelous facility with the English language to the work. Another translator was William Cole, an Oxford graduate who had fled to Zurich at the beginning of Mary's reign.

Anthony Gilby also helped with the translation. He was a Cambridge Hebrew scholar who had met Whittingham and Knox in Frankfurt. An outstanding preacher, he wrote numerous strongly worded tracts defending Calvin's teachings.

Still another translator was Thomas Sampson. Trained in law and divinity at Cambridge, he'd converted to Protestantism at the university. Although cantankerous, he was somewhat of a celebrity as a preacher and substituted for Knox when he was out of town. A radical Calvinist, he'd also fled to the Continent after Mary's accession. His first stop was Strasbourg, where he studied under John Tremellius, the Hebrew and Syrian Bible scholar who eventually put out the standard Protestant version of the Scriptures in Latin.

PUBLICATION OF THE GENEVA BIBLE

After the Protestant Queen Elizabeth came to the throne of England in 1558, most of the translators felt it was safe to go home. But Whittingham and a couple of others stayed in Geneva to finish the Bible that meant so much to them. According to its preface, they worked for "two years and more day and night" on the project. The completed Bible was published in 1560.

The Geneva Bible encouraged its radical Protestant readers in Scotland, Ireland, and England to fight back against persecution and strict government control. The title page, for instance, features a woodcut of a holy war, as well as this Bible quotation: "The Lord shal fight for you: therefore holde you your peace" (Ex. 14:14).

The Bible offered an extraordinary variety of study aids for the reader. For one thing, it was published in the handy quarto size

Title page of the Geneva Bible

(about nine by twelve inches). Most of the earlier English Bibles had been printed in the large and cumbersome cathedral size. Also, the Geneva text included verse divisions. The key subjects were marked by paragraph signs (¶). And there were "arguments" summarizing the main points in each book and chapter, as well as headnotes to guide the reader through the text. There were numerous marginal notes, mainly from Calvin's commentary. Another innovation was the easy-to-read roman type. The Bible also contained maps, an index and glossary, prayers, and rhyming psalms accompanied by music.

The Geneva Bible was the most accurate English translation yet produced, since the translators took full advantage of the spectacular array of new Bible scholarship available to them. Starting with the 1550 edition of the Great Bible as their base for the Old Testament, the translators consulted the Hebrew-Latin Bible of the Dominican scholar Santes Pagninus (1528), Estienne's Latin Bible (1557), the Hebrew Bible of German scholar Sebastian Münster (1534–35), and the just-revised French Bible of Calvin's cousin Olivétan. And, working from Whittingham's fine New Testament, the translators corrected the text with Beza's Latin Bible of 1556 and Estienne's Greek New Testament of 1551.

Roland Hall printed the Bible in Geneva. The printing costs came out of the pockets of the English exiles. Then the Bibles were smuggled into England.

CONTROVERSY OVER THE NEW BIBLE

The Geneva Bible instantly won the hearts of the English believers. For fifty years it would be the household Bible of Protestants in English-speaking countries. Yet, even though its translators had dedicated the Bible to Queen Elizabeth, she refused to authorize it as the official version of the English Church. But she later did allow the new Bible to be published and distributed in England—with her full knowledge and approval.

The queen had good reason for not setting her royal seal of approval on the Geneva Bible. First, it had been produced by a group whom she saw as rebel hotheads, since the exiles at Geneva had all opposed the royal prerogative of her sister, Mary. True, Elizabeth didn't agree with Mary's Catholic views, but she still insisted that a sovereign should be *obeyed,* no matter what. And she never forgave John Knox for writing a stinging tract claiming that women make poor monarchs! To strongly encourage a Bible put out by people who preached such stuff would be to encourage revolution.

Elizabeth had a further reason for objecting to the Geneva Bible. Its text, and especially its notes, were highly divisive. The comments on the Book of Revelation insulted Roman Catholics (and there were still many of them in England). These notes took every opportunity to say that the evil forces in Revelation—the dragon and so forth—really represented the pope and the Roman Church. But Elizabeth was committed to *uniting,* not dividing, her Church and her people. So she chose not to support a Bible that did so much to continue the warfare between Catholics and Protestants in her land.

The Geneva Bible was, in a sense, the Bible that the common people of England had always wanted. It was accurate, beautiful when read aloud, easy to use, and widely available. It gave the people Bible truth in language they could understand and carry with them in their hearts.

But the Geneva Bible was essentially a partisan Bible. Its notes and commentary, for all their scholarliness, were peppered with barbs and ill will. Elizabeth wanted a Bible that would confer the spirit of *blessing* on her people. So it would fall to her successor, James VI of Scotland, to bring such a Bible—the King James Bible—into being. And, in doing so, James and his translators would lean heavily on the Geneva Bible. They would take from it the best, and not the worst, that it had to offer.

CHAPTER SEVENTEEN

The Bishops' and Rheims-Douai Bibles: Forerunners of the King James Version

W hen Queen Elizabeth took the throne in 1558, England was, as we've said, a religious battleground. Ever since the reign of her father, Henry VIII, Protestants and Roman Catholics had been engaged in a virtual civil war. The war had started with Luther's reforms in Germany and spread quickly through Europe and into England. At the heart of this struggle was a conflict over the English-language Bible.

In the early days of her reign, all eyes had been focused on Elizabeth to see whether she'd come down on the side of the Protestants or the Catholics. As the Protestants gradually returned to England after Queen Mary's death, they had strong hopes that the new queen would embrace their cause—and their new Geneva Bible. Yet Elizabeth refused to give in to their demands. She wouldn't be pushed into authorizing the Geneva Bible, although she did grant a six-year license allowing for its publication.

At the same time, Elizabeth stood tenaciously behind the conservative Great Bible as the official church text, demanding that every parish church have a copy of it for the congregation to read. But the people had long since rejected the Great Bible. And they were passionately devoted to the Geneva text. Clearly, this situation posed a quandary for Elizabeth—one she called on her new Archbishop of Canterbury, Matthew Parker, to help her solve.

THE BISHOPS' BIBLE

Parker was a man Elizabeth trusted. He'd been a royal chaplain to her Protestant mother, Anne Boleyn. Advised by Parker, Elizabeth decided to chart a middle-of-the-road course for her Church. So Parker became the chief architect for implementing a compromise between warring Catholic and Protestant factions. Under his direction, the English bishops adopted a set of doctrinal principles known as the Thirty-nine Articles. These articles were general enough to provide a kind of umbrella—or "settlement"—under which all wings of the Church could gather.

The centerpiece of Parker's plan for unifying the Church was the publication of a new Bible. This idea actually had had its beginnings almost twenty years earlier, when Thomas Cranmer had proposed that the English bishops revise the unpopular Great Bible. At that time, the bishops had been unenthusiastic, and Cranmer complained that they probably wouldn't agree to such a project until "the day after doomsday."

But then, in 1561, Richard Cox, the radical Protestant bishop of Ely—who had supported the idea of a revision when Cranmer first proposed it—again suggested a new Bible. With Cox's support, Parker won approval for the idea from his bishops. The project probably didn't get under way until two or three years later, though, when the archbishop parceled out portions of the Bible to some of his bishops and to several qualified scholars.

Parker's directions were specific. His translators were to use the Great Bible as their basis, comparing it with the original Hebrew and Greek texts—as well as with the Latin Bibles of Santes Pagninus (a Dominican scholar who had translated the Bible out of the original Hebrew and Greek in 1518 and published it in 1528) and Sebastian Münster (who had translated the Hebrew Bible in 1534–1535). Most important of all, Parker's translators were to drop the "bitter [marginal] notes" that came from the Geneva Bible.

THE TRANSLATORS

From the very start, there was no question about who was in charge of the translation: it was Matthew Parker himself. He was the chief editor and coordinator. And he took on more of the actual translation work than any of his bishops—the Gospels of Matthew and Mark, and most of the Pauline epistles. He apparently didn't want to entrust the books that contained the heart of Christian doctrine to anyone but himself!

Parker was eminently qualified as a translator and loved scholarship. While at Cambridge, he'd studied the Bible and the Church Fathers. So, even though he was in poor health, he zealously took on the Bible project in addition to his many administrative duties as archbishop. He labored a total of seven years translating his portions of the Bible, as well as writing prefaces for the whole text, editing it, and preparing it for publication.

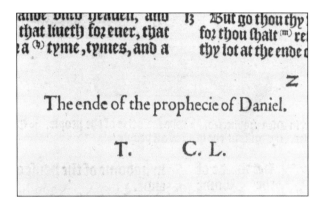

Detail of a page from the Bishops' Bible

Unfortunately, some of the other translators weren't as conscientious or as talented. They'd been chosen primarily because they were good churchmen (sooner or later all of them were made bishops)—and *not* because of their Bible scholarship. Because Parker wanted the people of England to be impressed by the august group of church officials who produced the Bible, he had each translator's initials printed at the end of the segment he'd worked on (see illustration).

Some of the translators, though, *were* well qualified. One of the most outstanding of these was William Alley, bishop of Exeter, who translated the book of Deuteronomy and possibly all of the Pentateuch. He'd completed his doctorate at Oxford in 1561 and written an excellent book on Hebrew grammar.

Another very capable translator was the Welshman Richard Davies, bishop of St. David's, whose stay in Geneva during Mary's reign had infused him with a passion to give the Bible to the people. When he returned to England after Elizabeth became queen, Davies finished his doctorate at Oxford and went on to sponsor the first translation of the Bible into Welsh. In the Bishops' Bible, he translated Joshua through II Samuel. His fellow translator on the Welsh Bible, Gabriel Goodman, dean of Westminster Abbey, prepared I Corinthians for the Bishops' text.

Some of the translator-bishops were strong Puritans—like Edwin Sandys of Worcester and Thomas Bentham, who had risked his life ministering to the Protestants in London during Queen Mary's reign. Others—like Richard Cox of Ely and William Barlow of Chichester—were high Anglicans who had wanted for a long time to revise the Bible.

Overall, the most remarkable thing about the translators was that they represented such a range of religious viewpoints. Some were Catholic sympathizers, others were Puritans, and others were moderate. But because the translators didn't *confer*, or work together as a committee, the Bishops' Bible turned out to be woefully inconsistent—in voice, in accuracy, in literary style.

Virtually all the translators were preachers, and their sense of oratory gave the Bishops' text some lovely and memorable turns of phrase. On the other hand, the Bible quickly came under fire for stilted and amateurish wordings, such as the following, from Psalm 46, verses 1 and 2: "The Lorde is our refuge and strength: a helpe very easyly founde in troubles. Therfore we wyll not feare though the earth be transposed: and though the hilles rushe into the middest of the sea."

"SELLING" THE BIBLE TO THE PUBLIC

When the Bishops' Bible finally came out in 1568, Parker did all he could to package it attractively. He had it sumptuously printed and bound by Richard Jugge, the royal printer, using the same easy-to-read roman type the Geneva had featured. Also, he transferred into it

Spine of the Bishops' Bible

some of the less controversial notes from the Geneva text and even picked up some of the wordings from that Bible. There were numerous Geneva-like readers' aids as well, including maps, illustrations, and elaborate genealogical charts.

The title page displayed a flattering portrait of Elizabeth. Next came Parker's preface, urging the reader to "Searche . . . as Christe byddeth thee the holy scriptures, wherein thou mayest finde thy salvation." Finally, Parker included Archbishop Thomas Cranmer's much-beloved endorsement of Bible reading, taken from the "Cranmer" edition of the Great Bible.

Despite all these efforts, though, the Bishops' Bible was unpopular from the start. The public recognized it as little more than a warmed-over version of the Great Bible. It lacked the scholarship, readability, and beauty of the Geneva Bible. No wonder most rank-and-file English men and women persisted in reading the black-market Geneva Bible in their homes, even though they had to listen to the newly authorized Bishops' Bible at church!

Parker apparently saw no reason why ordinary men and women had to have the Bible at home for private study. So he flatly refused to release the Bishops' text in the convenient and inexpensive quarto and octavo sizes that the people loved. He clearly felt it was enough for worshipers to hear the Bible read at *church* services—and to stand in line for a quick look at the one huge, cathedral-size Bible that each church was required to have on the premises, chained usually to a large desk or stand.

It wasn't until Parker's death in 1575 that his stranglehold on Bible publication was broken. Just three weeks after his passing, seven of Elizabeth's top advisers got together to commission a new edition of the Geneva Bible. From that time on, editions of the Geneva Bible rolled off the queen's presses at a steady clip—soon outnumbering the Bishops' Bible editions by a ratio of nearly *nine to one!*

Cover of the first edition of the Bishops' Bible, 1568

Title page of the Bishops' Bible

THE RHEIMS-DOUAI BIBLE

As soon as it became clear to Roman Catholics that Elizabeth was determined to steer her Church in a Protestant direction, they fled the country in droves. They were horrified that she'd allowed some three hundred Catholics to be executed. Then in 1568, the year the Bishops' Bible was published, a group of these militant English Catholics established a college in Douai, France, to educate priests who, they hoped, would reconvert England to Catholicism.

The founder of this college was William Allen, an Oxford graduate who'd left England for France under pressure from Elizabeth's government. In France, he was

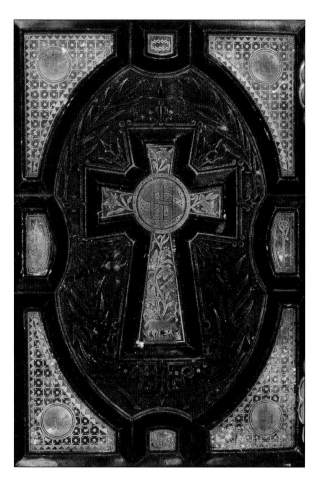

Cover detail of Rheims-Douai Bible, 1875

ordained a priest and gathered around him a group of brilliant Catholic scholars—graduates of Oxford and Cambridge—as faculty members. Allen himself then earned a doctorate from the college and became a professor of divinity there.

When Pope Pius V excommunicated Elizabeth in 1570, he told English Catholics that they no longer had to obey the queen. He even encouraged foreign monarchs like Philip II of Spain to overthrow Elizabeth's government. Allen fit right in with this scheme, working closely with the next pope, Gregory XIII, and with Philip II—both of whom heavily subsidized the college—in developing plots to replace Elizabeth with a Catholic monarch. For her part, the queen denounced both the seminary and the Jesuits who took over the college after 1573.

A crucial part of Allen's plan to reconvert his native land to Catholicism was the idea of a new English Bible—a Bible that would maintain a strictly Catholic point of view. He chose Gregory Martin, Douai's leading Bible scholar, to take on the task of translating *the entire Bible.* Martin, an Oxford graduate, was an authority on Biblical languages.

Martin began with the Old Testament in 1578, completing two chapters a day. And, in spite of rapidly declining health, he pressed on until he completed the New Testament just weeks before his death in 1582. The New Testament was published later that year in Rheims, where the college had moved temporarily to avoid harassment by Protestant spies from England. The college didn't have the funds to publish Martin's Old Testament until 1609–1610, when the entire Bible was renamed the Rheims-Douai version.

William Allen and Richard Bristow, another Oxford-trained Bible scholar, helped Martin put together the prefaces and notes for the Bible. Bristow, like Martin, gave the translation his last supreme efforts before his death in 1581. Another scholar who helped was William Rainolds, an Oxford man who taught Hebrew and divinity at the Catholic seminary.

The introduction to the Rheims New Testament, probably written by Allen, explains that Gregory Martin didn't really approve of translating the Bible into ordinary spoken languages. And, Allen says, the ancient Church Fathers were against giving the Bible to just anyone. They felt it needed to be *explained by church officials* before people could understand it.

So why, in view of all this, were the Roman Catholics publishing the Bible in English? Only because, Allen explains, the Protestants have already given the Bible to English-speaking people. And the Protestants, in Allen's opinion, have badly *botched* their Bibles. So, he says, it's up to good Catholics to do the job correctly—without bias or faulty scholarship.

Allen goes on to say in his preface that the Rheims Bible is based on the Latin Vulgate Bible, rather than on the original Hebrew and Greek texts. And he goes to considerable lengths to defend that decision, explaining proudly that the Rheims translators have given a word-for-word rendering from the Vulgate—a rendering that features some specially made up *Latin-English* words based on the sacred Vulgate text.

RECEPTION OF THE RHEIMS NEW TESTAMENT

All in all, this theory of translation produced a Bible that was sometimes graceful and meaningful but often awkward and unintelligible because of its literal renderings and strange-sounding Latinized words. These Latin-based words—like *supersubstantial* for *daily* (Matt. 6:11); *supererogate* for *spendest more* (Luke 10:35); and *prefinition* for *eternal* (Eph. 3:11)—made little sense to English readers.

So far as the English Church was concerned, the Rheims Bible's most serious flaw was the stinging anti-Protestant bias of its marginal notes. As a modern Catholic historian has pointed out, these notes contain "a veritable catechism of Christian doctrine" as given from the Roman Catholic point of view.

To Elizabeth, the Rheims New Testament was a vicious attack on her royal prerogative. She was quite aware that it was part of a scheme to overthrow her government. And a Puritan theologian named William Fulke was so incensed with the Rheims text that he published a side-by-side edition of the Rheims and Bishops' New Testaments, designed to prove how inferior the Catholic text was. But instead of exposing the weaknesses of the *Rheims* text, Fulke's publication served to point out the deficiencies of the *Bishops'* text. And it showed off the virtues of the Rheims Bible. So, to Fulke's and Elizabeth's horror, the parallel edition ended up popularizing the illegal and subversive Roman Catholic New Testament!

By the end of the sixteenth century, the Bishops' Bible—the one authorized version of Scripture available to the English people—was running a distant third in public opinion behind the Geneva Bible and the Rheims New Testament. As Elizabeth's reign came to a close in 1603, there was a virtual deadlock in Bible publication. The people had clearly rejected the Bishops' Bible in favor of the Geneva Bible and the Rheims New Testament. This placed both the church hierarchy and the queen in an untenable position. They were doggedly standing behind a Bible that almost *no one* read. And they were condemning Bibles that just about *everyone* read.

One thing was clear. No existing Bible was meeting the needs of all the people in England. The Geneva and Rheims Bibles were too extremist, and the Bishops' Bible was too conservative. It was natural, therefore, that certain visionaries should begin to think of translating a *new* Bible—one that could please *everybody*. One of these visionaries was James VI of Scotland, a distant cousin of Elizabeth who was standing in the wings, hoping the queen would name him as her successor.

A paramount reason James wanted to be king was so he could carry out a project that had long been dear to his heart—the translation of a new and ecumenical English Bible. He wanted a chance to succeed in something Elizabeth had failed at—finding a Bible that could unite the warring religious factions in England. To do this, James must have known he'd have to build on strong foundations—the Geneva, the Bishops', and the Rheims Bibles. So it would be the task of James and his translators to weave these three texts together with other great Scriptural texts of the past to form a new Bible—one that would endure long after its predecessors had been forgotten.

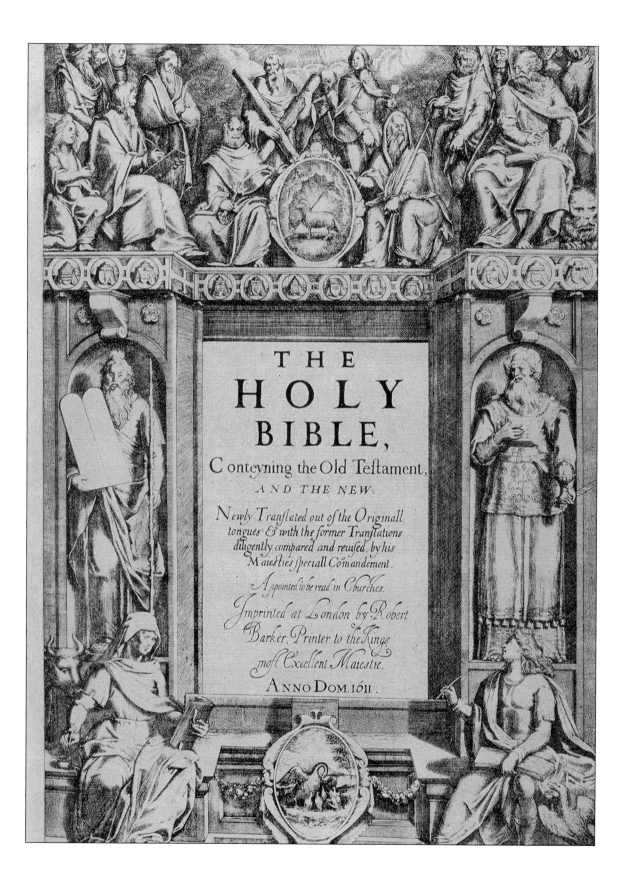

THE HOLY BIBLE,

Conteyning the Old Testament,

AND THE NEW.

Newly Translated out of the Originall tongues: & with the former Translations diligently compared and reuised, by his Maiesties speciall Comandement.

Appointed to be read in Churches.

Imprinted at London by Robert Barker, Printer to the Kings most Excellent Maiestie.

ANNO DOM. 1611.

VIII

THE KING JAMES BIBLE: THE CROWN OF ENGLISH LITERATURE

CHAPTER EIGHTEEN

King James Commissions His Bible

A t ten o'clock in the morning on March 24, 1603–just hours after Queen Elizabeth's passing–King James VI of Scotland, heir to the British throne, became King James I of England. Within hours, well-wishers from across the entire religious and political spectrum rushed northward to the Scottish border to greet the new king. Calvinists, Roman Catholics, and middle-of-the-road Anglicans all wanted to be the first to congratulate him–and to ask him for special favors.

James didn't disappoint his new subjects. As he and his royal entourage moved slowly into England, the scene was one of ecstatic celebration. Thrilled with his newly acquired royal office, James loved nothing better than to grant favors. Between Edinburgh and London he conferred more than three hundred knighthoods, handed out hundreds of new appointments, granted countless petitions, and gave away untold sums of money and packets of the Crown's land.

Some of the petitions presented to James stood no chance of being granted. For instance, the Catholics, who had been sorely oppressed under Elizabeth, asked the king to allow them to practice their religion freely. And some Puritan radicals appealed to James to remove the bishops in the Anglican Church and to usher in a democratic, Calvinist-style organization. Only *one* of the numerous religious petitions James received at this point seemed reasonable to him–the Puritans' Millenary Petition.

THE MILLENARY PETITION

It was probably at Sir Oliver Cromwell's estate in Hinchingbrook–where the good knight entertained the king lavishly on his way southward–that three influential Puritan ministers presented James

*King James VI of Scotland,
who became King James I
of England*

with the Millenary Petition. It had been signed by close to a thousand (*millenary* means "thousand") highly respectable ministers and had the backing of Puritan leaders all over the land.

The Millenarists' requests were mild. They simply asked for an ecumenical meeting between the church bishops and the Puritans, so that "things amisse in our Church" could be decided once and for all—with the king acting as judge. They wanted to talk about practices that were of concern to many churchmen, such as using the sign of the cross in baptism, the requirement that ministers wear special vestments, the fact that many ministers didn't preach sermons to their congregations (some never even went near their churches!), and the reading of the Apocrypha in church services.

James was immediately sympathetic with the Millenary Petition and let the Puritans know he'd grant them a "conference." Later, he announced that the meeting would be held at the royal palace at Hampton Court, some ten miles west of London, on January 14, 1604.

But as the meeting date for the Hampton Court Conference drew near, James had to reassure all parties involved. The bishops were afraid the new king would give in to *all* the Puritan demands—and maybe even abolish the church hierarchy altogether. The Puritans, on the other hand, were afraid James would publicly embarrass them by refusing to grant *any* of their requests. No one knew exactly where James stood on these issues. He was a man of many moods, a man amazingly tolerant of both Puritans and Catholics (in fact, his wife was a Catholic), a man who was at heart a compromiser and a peacemaker.

One thing was for sure. He saw the upcoming conference as an unmissable opportunity to launch a project he felt was crucially important to his success as king—the translation of a new version of the English Bible.

JAMES: BIBLE SCHOLAR
AND PEACEMAKER

James's upbringing in Scotland was unusual, to say the least. When he was scarcely a year old, he became king of that country—thanks to the abdication of his mother, Mary, Queen of Scots. She'd been forced out of office and imprisoned following a scandal that had connected her with her husband's murder. Mary's political enemies had been concerned about something else—the fact that she was a devout Roman Catholic. So they saw to it that the young king was separated from his mother and raised by strict Calvinist guardians, the earl of Mar and his wife.

The earl hired a team of brilliant and impassioned Calvinist scholars to educate James. Chief among these tutors were George Buchanan and Peter Young, who felt that the better James understood the Bible, the more effective he'd someday be as king. So, from the time James was four years old, they subjected him to a twice-daily routine of linguistic, theological, and scientific studies that included Bible reading in Latin, Greek, Hebrew, English, and French. By the time he was eight, James could translate any Bible passage from Latin into French, and from French into English, with ease.

When James took the reins of the Scottish government as a teenager in 1582, he had to tread a fine line between the Calvinistic Presbyterians of the powerful Scottish Kirk (Church) and the Catholic nobility. He did this by stepping aside from his Calvinist upbringing and becoming a dedicated peacemaker—a promoter of national religious unity—who was careful not to offend *any* religious group.

The young king leaned heavily, too, on the words of Scripture as his guidebook to kingship. And later, James advised his son Prince Henry to study the Bible. "All my Religion," he told him, "presently professed by me and my kingdome was grounded upon the plaine words of Scripture, without the which all points of Religion are superfluous."

But James wasn't above quoting Scripture to his own political advantage. As a matter of fact, he wrote a book called *The Trew Law of Free Monarchies*, in which he cites numerous passages of Scripture to prove that the office of king was "founded by God himself."

James was too politically smart to take sides in the tug-of-war over Bible versions. He knew that if he endorsed the Calvinist Geneva Bible, he'd offend Catholics, and if he endorsed the Rheims or Bishops' Bible, he'd offend the Kirk. He proposed, therefore, an entirely *new* translation of Scripture to the General Assembly of the Kirk in 1601. The assembly ignored his suggestion.

James could only look forward to the day when he'd be king of England. Perhaps then he'd be able to persuade the Anglican bishops to translate a new Bible—an *ecumenical* Bible that would unite Protestants and Catholics in Scotland and England. But, secretly, James hoped his new Bible would accomplish something more. He hoped it would somehow make him the great peacemaker of Europe and guarantee for warring religious factions everywhere a worldwide reign of "Beautiful Peace."

PARTICIPANTS IN THE HAMPTON COURT CONFERENCE

James handpicked the four Puritan representatives who attended the conference at Hampton Court, inviting only men who would support the Anglican Church. He excluded extremists who would oppose the kind of compromise needed to unify the Church. And the four Puritans that James invited were all strong Bible scholars—men who would favor a fresh translation of the English Bible. In fact, two of them—John Rainolds and Laurence Chaderton—later played prominent roles in the King James translation.

The foreman of the Puritan delegation was Rainolds, leader of the Puritan movement at Oxford. A former Roman Catholic, Rainolds was the brother of William Rainolds, who had helped prepare the Rheims-Douai Bible. John Rainolds was a renowned university lecturer, writer, and preacher, as well as a master of Greek grammar and rhetoric—known for being "wholly addicted . . . to the study of the holy Scriptures."

Chaderton headed up the radical Protestant movement at Cambridge. He was always in trouble with church officials for violating ceremonial traditions at the Puritan Emmanuel College, where he was master. But he was a lovable compromiser who was at heart a mainline Anglican. And Chaderton was a towering Bible scholar who

Hampton Court Palace, as it appears today

spent countless hours studying Latin, Hebrew, and Greek. He then turned this knowledge into passionate and down-to-earth sermons that moved his listeners to tears.

The other two Puritans invited to the conference, John Knew-stubb and Thomas Sparke, were also prominent university men. Knewstubb had written a number of Puritan tracts directed against what he regarded as extremist groups, like the Roman Catholics and the "Family of Love." Sparke, too, wrote controversial pamphlets against the Catholics. But neither man let his opinions get in the way of his loyalty to the Anglican Church. And both men were ardent students of the Bible.

To counterbalance the Puritan contingent at the Hampton Court Conference, James summoned Archbishop of Canterbury John Whitgift, eight bishops, and ten other high-ranking officials of the English Church. Although most of these men were hearty opponents of Puritanism, they were open to correcting "things amisse in the Church."

A number of these church officials were strong Bible scholars, and undoubtedly open to the idea of a new translation of Scripture. Fully *seven* of them later joined the King James Bible translation team. Archbishop Whitgift had for years wanted a new Bible, though he'd been unable to get Queen Elizabeth's support for the project. Another church official concerned about the future of the English Bible was Bishop Thomas Bilson, who was indignant over what he called "the vaine shew made" by the Roman Catholics in their Rheims New Testament. Bishop John Overall was an internationally known Hebrew scholar and expert on the Babylonian captivity.

Then, of course, there was the great Lancelot Andrewes, dean of Westminster Abbey. Andrewes had been awarded one of the very first scholarships in Greek and Hebrew to be offered at Cambridge, and he was famous for also knowing Latin, Chaldean, Syriac, and Arabic—in addition to some fifteen modern languages. Andrewes saw the futility of staying with the Bishops' Bible. So, in his stunningly metaphysical sermons, he had long ago abandoned using the Bishops' text in favor of the Geneva version and his own original translations of Scripture.

Perhaps more than anyone else present at the conference, Andrewes would have appreciated the king's dream of an ecumenical Bible. He was at heart as much of a peacemaker as the king. He saw no reason why fellow Christians should fight over doctrine and once wrote: "If conscience were made of that which is out of controversy, of that only which is elemental to Christian salvation, a way of peace then there shall be whereof all parts shall agree, even in the midst of a world of controversies." There was no doubt that Andrewes was King James's favorite preacher. And it was well known that the king usually slept with one of Andrewes' sermons under his pillow.

THE CONFERENCE BEGINS

On the eve of the conference, James held a small reception for all the participants. Some of them had been at Hampton Court for the past month or so, celebrating the Christmas holidays with the king and filling the palace's twelve hundred rooms with Yuletide pageantry and joy. Just a few days earlier, Shakespeare had presented one of his plays to the assembled guests.

The first day of the conference, all the participants met in the royal privy chamber. After brief opening remarks, the king unceremoniously excluded the four Puritan representatives from the whole day's activities. He then took aside the church officials and conferred with them privately about the Puritan "complaints." To everyone's surprise, James argued in *favor* of most of these complaints and, as Andrewes later said, "wonderfully played the Puritan." He won clear victories for the Puritans on several major points.

The second day of the conference, the Puritans were finally allowed to enter the discussion. They shocked everyone by wearing Turkish robes in place of their scholastic garb. This was an obvious protest against university and church traditions. According to an eyewitness report, James gave them a "pithy and sweet speech" and invited them to present their case.

Immediately, John Rainolds—spokesman for the group—dropped to his knees and pleaded the Puritan cause, summarizing all the points in the Millenary Petition. James was impatient with Rainolds, but gave in to many of the Puritan demands. The king agreed to major modifications in the Book of Common Prayer and the church liturgy. Only three of the Puritans' requests met with out-and-out rejection.

The Anglican response to Rainolds's presentation was sharp. Bishop Bancroft of London attacked Rainolds repeatedly, defending church ceremonies and hierarchy. James, too, insulted Rainolds's group, calling their demands "very idle and frivolous." He probably, however, did this to impress the bishops present.

The King James version of Psalms

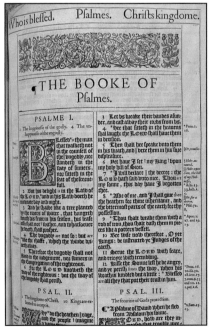

A NEW BIBLE IS CALLED FOR

Finally, as James talked of the need for unanimity and peacemaking within the Church, Rainolds saw an opportunity to propose a project dear to his own heart—"a *newe* translation of the *Bible.*" Then he pointed out that such a move would be politically advantageous to James. Rainolds went on to cite several *mis*translations in previous English Bibles, showing how each one had encouraged civil disobedience—the thing he knew James feared the most.

One mistranslation Rainolds cited was from Psalms 105:28, where the original meaning of the Greek ("They were not disobedient") praises the Israelites for obeying God even when He inflicted trials on them in Egypt. According

Title page of New Testament from the first edition of the King James Bible, 1611

Detail of I Corinthians 13:13 from the first edition of the King James Bible

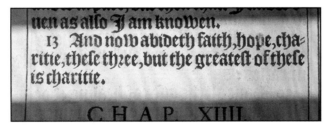

to Rainolds, the Bishops' translation actually *inverts* the correct reading and states that the Jews "were not obedient." To James, such a mistranslation would have been downright treasonous, implying that a person doesn't have to obey God—and the king as God's earthly representative—under certain circumstances.

Bishop Bancroft quickly objected to Rainolds's proposal for a new Bible, grumbling that "if every man's humour should be followed, there would be no ende of translating." But when he saw that the king agreed with Rainolds, Bancroft said nothing more on the subject.

For his part, James let everyone know he thought the new Bible was a wonderful idea. He made it clear he didn't like any of the previous English Bibles, though he felt the Geneva text was the "worst of all." Its notes, he said, were "seditious," "daungerous," and "trayterous." And he went on to cite several Geneva notes that encouraged "disobedience to Kings."

Then, not five minutes after Rainolds had suggested a new Bible, the king commanded that "one uniforme translation" be begun at once. And, as if he'd already planned it, he outlined on the spot the precise way his order was to be carried out. "This is to be done," he said, "by the best learned in both the Universities [Oxford and Cambridge], after them to bee reviewed by the Bishops, and the chiefe learned in the Church." He went on to say that the new Bible should next "bee presented to the Privie-Councell; and lastly ... bee ratified by his Royall authoritie."

James managed to please almost everyone with this plan. The university men, the church officials, and the privy councillors were undoubtedly all happy to be included in the translation process. And James himself must have been delighted that he'd have the final word in editing the new translation.

Next, the king explained that he expected the new Bible to accomplish two important objectives. First, it would help him unite the badly divided English Church. Second, it would help secure his royal prerogative, his hold on the government of England. With these objectives in mind, he specifically stated that the new Bible and its notes should support the institutions of kingship and church organization.

As James closed the conference the following day, he talked only of church unity and brotherhood—speaking so movingly that participants on both sides wept. And his words weren't empty of meaning. During the next calendar year, he proved just how sincere he was about national religious unity by driving the ambitious Bible project forward with almost incredible speed and energy. Step by step, he followed through on his Hampton Court plans to launch a new Bible. He set both Puritans and Anglicans, liberals and conservatives, university and church leaders to work, shoulder to shoulder, on "one uniforme translation" of the Bible. And in doing so, he kept alive something very special—the ecumenical spirit of Hampton Court.

CHAPTER NINETEEN

The King James Translation: Setting the Great Work in Motion

Y ou will scarcely conceive howe earnest his Majestie is to have this worke begonne." These were the words that Richard Bancroft, Archbishop of Canterbury and director of the King James Bible translation, wrote in his letter to officials at Cambridge University in July of 1604—just six months after James had commissioned the new Bible at the Hampton Court Conference.

From the very start, the king was "the principal Mover and Author of the work," as the translators themselves wrote in the dedication and preface to the completed King James Version. It was he alone who—in their words—propelled the design for the new Bible forward "that the work might be hastened, and that the business might be expedited in so decent a manner, as a matter of such importance might justly require."

James was confident, as we've mentioned earlier, that a new Bible could somehow unite the English Church, splintered as it was into rival factions, ranging from high-church Anglicans to low-church Puritans. So he continually pressured—and inspired—the bishops, the universities, and Secretary of State Robert Cecil until they'd completed the maze of preliminary arrangements for the translation—and until the six committees of Bible scholars had set their hands to the momentous and holy task of rethinking, rewording, and refashioning the English Bible.

BANCROFT PICKED TO COORDINATE
THE BIBLE PROJECT

At the Hampton Court Conference—where the Puritans had petitioned the king for a new translation of the English Bible—Bancroft (then bishop of London) had said flatly that there was no need for another English Bible. But that was before he knew how passionately the king wanted a new Bible. As soon as he saw that, Bancroft did an about-face and became one of the principal champions of the translation. When the king, in turn, saw Bancroft's enthusiasm for the project, he quickly appointed him general coordinator of it *and* named him Archbishop of Canterbury.

Right after the king's coronation, in mid-March of 1604, James, Bancroft, and Cecil threw themselves into launching the translation process. First, Bancroft asked Lancelot Andrewes, dean of Westminster, as well as Edward Lively and John Harding, the Regius (royal) professors at Cambridge and Oxford, to be regional supervisors for three translation teams—to be based in London, Cambridge, and Oxford, respectively. Each team was to be divided into two committees—one made up of Hebrew scholars and the other of Greek scholars.

Then the archbishop asked the three supervisors to submit lists of outstanding Greek and Hebrew scholars to serve as translators. James approved the lists from all three supervisors without a single change.

INSTRUCTIONS FROM THE KING

In July, James wrote Bancroft with a set of detailed guidelines on how the translation process should work. In this letter, he first orders Bancroft to invite virtually *any Hebrew or Greek scholar in the land* to offer "observations," or suggestions, for the various translation committees to consider in their work. Then the king goes on to announce the makeup of the six translation committees—three Hebrew committees to work on the Old Testament and three Greek committees to work on the New Testament. The list adds up to some fifty-four translators in all—the largest translation team ever assembled to date for an English-language Bible!

The king also encloses in his letter a set of "Rules to be observ'd in Translation of the Bible." In the "Rules," James tries to please *everyone*—from high-church Anglicans to low-church Puritans. But more than that, his instructions virtually ensure that no extremist group—high Anglican or Puritan—can take over the translation process. This would help guarantee a fair and accurate result: a Bible that would be true to the original Hebrew and Greek texts.

Of course, high churchmen would have found much to be delighted about in the "Rules." The rules require, for instance, that the translators follow the conservative Bishops' Bible text and leave it "as little altered, as the truth of the Originall will permitt." Also, they require the translators to stay with old ecclesiastical words like *Church,* instead of using the more democratic-sounding *congregation.* The scholars are to choose wordings that agree with the Church Fathers and traditional Anglican theology. And they're to eliminate *all controversial marginal notes* except those that explain the original Hebrew or Greek meanings.

But there was also plenty in the king's rules to encourage the *Puritans*—to assure them that the king's new Bible wouldn't take on an overly conservative point of view. For instance, James makes it clear that the new Bible should be a *translation,* not just a revision of the old Bishops' text. "Evry particular man of evry companie," James says, is first to translate each chapter by himself. Then he's to meet with his whole committee to "agree" democratically on the best wording for that chapter. If agreement isn't possible, the other translation committees are to review the passage. And if *they* can't agree on a wording, the dispute goes to a "genrall meeting," where representatives from all the committees are to make a final recommendation.

Puritans must also have been pleased to see one further provision in the king's "Rules"—permission to consult the radical Protestant Bibles of the past—the Tyndale, Matthew's, and Geneva texts. This decision ensured that the beauty, poetry, and evangelical power of those beloved Bibles wouldn't be lost. The best that these Bibles had to offer would be, once and for all, incorporated into the national version of Scripture.

FINANCIAL ARRANGEMENTS

Financing the new Bible posed a major predicament for James. His treasury was under tremendous strain. So he had to turn to other resources: the church coffers, the universities, and the generosity of the translators themselves.

On July 22, James wrote Bancroft ordering him to levy a royal surcharge on the English clergy to fund the translation. The letter tells the archbishop, too, to redirect the salaries from all vacant ministerial posts to the "learned men" serving as translators. On the same date, James wrote Secretary Cecil, telling him to instruct the universities to provide room and board for the translators working at Oxford and Cambridge.

As it turned out, these financial arrangements were woefully inadequate. Church officials contributed nothing to the project. The universities proved a bit more generous, though, and some of the Cambridge colleges even offered a small stipend to the translators. But, on the whole, most of the "learned men" who took part in the project grappled with poverty during the six to eight years it took to produce the King James Bible. They labored out of sheer love for the Holy Scriptures—and for their fellow countrymen.

THE TRANSLATION WORK BEGINS

On July 31, 1604, Bancroft—speaking on behalf of the king—wrote the supervisors at Oxford, Cambridge, and Westminster, telling them to begin the translation at once. So that "no tyme may be overslipped by yowe for the better furtherance of this Holy worke," he said, all the translators should assemble immediately to "addresse themselves forthwith to this busyness" and to do so "with all possible spede."

PROFILE OF THE TRANSLATORS AS A WHOLE

In their careful selection of translators, the three regional directors (Lancelot Andrewes at Westminster, John Harding at Oxford, and Edward Lively at Cambridge) were supremely ecumenical. Their prime criterion was scholarship in Greek, Hebrew, and Latin—without apparent regard for the translators' theological point of view.

By including Anglicans of all types—high churchmen, low churchmen, and moderates—on each of the six committees, the directors welcomed healthy controversy into the translation process. They felt that, just as the full color spectrum blends to a neutral gray, the full theological range would coalesce into moderation.

Though only a handful of the translators admitted publicly to being Puritans, almost half of them could be classified as moderates with strong low-church, or Calvinist, leanings. Then there were the Arminians—a small but influential number of translators who believed in the doctrine of "free will" (considered heresy by the Church). The remaining translators were moderate to conservative high churchmen. This breadth of representation on the various committees virtually guaranteed at the outset that extremists would cancel each other out, thus allowing the middle-Anglican majority to prevail.

The translators included the elite of university Biblical scholars. Nearly three quarters of them, approximately thirty-five, had at some time taught on the university level. Among the Oxford translators, six were present or future Regius professors. Five were present or future college masters (presidents). The Cambridge men were equally impressive. Seven were or would be Regius professors, and eight college masters. Most held doctorates.

United in their general Anglicanism, in their loyalty to the king, and in their love for Scripture, the translators were sustained through arduous years of work together by their unflagging zeal for the idea of giving a new and totally unbiased version of the Bible to the English people. Notes on the committee procedures by one of the translators show that there were hot clashes among them. But the important thing is that the translators *subordinated* these personal differences to their common goal.

Unquestionably, an appointment as one of the fifty-four translators was a high honor. Writing in 1614 to the bishop of Bath and Wells to request a promotion, Samuel Ward lists as the final and most impressive of his four principal qualifications this simple fact—"I was a translator."

THUMBNAIL SKETCHES OF THE
SIX COMMITTEES

The Westminster Hebrew Committee–Translators of Genesis through II Kings. Lancelot Andrewes was a brilliant choice as chairman of this committee. He had an astounding grasp of Hebrew, Greek, Latin, Chaldaic, Syriac, and Aramaic, as well as some fifteen vernacular languages. And he was so well grounded in his

West front of Westminster Abbey

knowledge of the Church Fathers that his friends often compared him with "those virtuous men." He was an international clearinghouse for Bible scholarship in England and on the Continent. And, in an age of great sermon writing, his sermons were unsurpassed.

Andrewes's nine committee members included two outspoken Arminians; divinity scholar Hadrian Saravia; an adventurer named John Layfield, who had been a chaplain in the West Indies and written a popular book on his travels; and William Bedwell, who had founded Arabic studies in England.

Andrewes, a restrained and tolerant man, was supremely qualified to mediate between the various factions on his committee. In making him chairman of the Westminster Hebrew group, James and Bancroft placed the Pentateuch in the hands of a literary master.

The Cambridge Hebrew Committee–Translators of I Chronicles through Song of Solomon. This committee included some of the foremost Hebrew experts in England. Its chairman was Edward Lively–a moderate Anglican who had chosen marriage and thirteen children over university advancement. Lively had written the outstanding Hebrew grammar book of the day and was convinced that one has to return to the original Hebrew texts to grasp the teachings of the Old Testament. He would naturally have wanted the new Bible to be a fresh translation from the Hebrew.

His untimely death in 1605 threw Lively's committee into temporary confusion. Yet the impress of his thinking remained with both Cambridge committees, since he'd been general overseer of the entire group and had appointed all its translators.

After Lively's passing, John Richardson stepped into the committee chairmanship. Richardson probably kept his radical Arminian views to himself, deferring instead to the much-beloved Laurence Chaderton, a national leader of the Puritan movement.

Chaderton would have been to the Cambridge group the spiritual and intellectual fountainhead that Lancelot Andrewes was to the Westminster group. And, as father of the evangelical preaching style in England, Chaderton must have been a priceless workman in the great poetic books of the Bible—Psalms, Proverbs, Song of Solomon, and Ecclesiastes.

St. John's College, Cambridge University

Other members of the committee included the poet Thomas Harrison and the popular writer Francis Dillingham.

The Oxford Hebrew Committee–Translators of Isaiah through Malachi. Chairman John Harding was Regius professor of Hebrew at Oxford. He was a Puritan and had named several like-minded scholars to his committee. So, wisely perhaps, Bancroft assigned to this radical group an important but noncontroversial section of the Bible–the majestic and poetic voices of the great Hebrew prophets.

Christ Church College, Oxford University

The guiding spirit of the committee was the ardent Calvinist John Rainolds, who had initiated the whole translation project at the Hampton Court Conference. Although Rainolds was gravely ill, he persisted stead-fastly with the work. The other committee members came to his apartment at Corpus Christi College once a week to work with him at his bedside, until his death in 1607.

Rainolds's scholarship was considered "little less than miracu-lous" in all fields–particularly in Hebrew and Oriental linguistics. And it was especially appropriate that a man whose every sermon touched on the subject of sin should direct the translation of Israelite prophets like Jeremiah and Amos, who were so deeply distressed over the sins of *their* people.

Other translators on this committee included Regius Divinity Professor Thomas Holland, the popular Puritan preacher Richard Kilbye, and Miles Smith (known as a "walking library" for his knowl-edge of Chaldaic, Syriac, Arabic, Hebrew, Greek, Latin, and geography).

The Cambridge Greek-Hebrew Committee–Translators of the Apocrypha. Of the six committee members translating the Apocrypha, at least three were low churchmen who probably saw the Apocrypha as less than the Word of God. They may even have wanted to eliminate it from the new Bible. So Bancroft picked a strong churchman, John Duport, to chair the group. As two-time vice chancellor at Cambridge, Duport had developed a reputation for strict discipline and haranguing against "Disorders in the University."

Duport's main supporter on the committee was probably Andrew Downes, a high churchman who was considered the leading Greek scholar of the period. Another outstanding committee member was Downes's star pupil, John Bois, who—as a junior faculty member—may well have been the workhorse of the committee. A popular minister known for his polished sermons, Bois was something of a dynamo. He worked almost round the clock, beginning his Hebrew and Greek lectures at four o'clock in the morning.

Committee member Samuel Ward, master of Sidney Sussex College, was a passionate Puritan famous for educating some of the great preachers of the age. His feeling for style must have given the King James Apocrypha much of its dramatic power. And, as a lifelong peacemaker, he must have poured healing balm on the discussion in a committee that might otherwise have turned into a theological battleground.

The Oxford Greek Committee—Translators of the Gospels, Acts, and Revelation. Bancroft assigned the books containing the heart of Jesus' teachings to a committee with a careful balance of high churchmen and low churchmen. To guide the group in its work, he chose as chairman the staunch high Anglican Thomas Ravis, known at Oxford as an excellent administrator and a no-nonsense disciplinarian who sometimes locked up students for misbehaving. Ravis, who had objected to the idea of the new translation at first, probably wanted to stay close to the old Bishops' Bible wording.

Yet several liberal committee members, especially the feisty Puritan George Abbot, might have challenged Ravis's conservatism. Abbot was never much of a Bible scholar, but he was so devoted to the Crown, the Church, and the Bible that James eventually appointed him Archbishop of Canterbury. And he had a wonderful knack with words—with preaching and writing in good, clear English.

There were also four extremely competent Greek scholars on the committee. The most outstanding of these was Eton College Provost Sir Henry Savile, who had an awesome international reputation as translator and educator.

The Westminster Greek Committee–Translators of Romans through Jude. This committee may have posed a particular challenge for Bancroft. Only three of the seven members were strong Greek scholars, and all three had a Puritan/Calvinist turn of thought. This, Bancroft may have feared, might give a definite slant to the heart of Paul's teaching.

Bancroft solved this problem by appointing church conservative William Barlow as committee chairman. The archbishop knew that Barlow–as the ranking churchman and only published author on the committee–would be able to stand up to the Puritans.

The committee members had many strengths. Barlow was an effective tract and sermon writer. Roger Fenton was a compelling popular preacher. And John Spencer was the talented editor of Richard Hooker's famous *Laws of Ecclesiastical Polity.*

Above all, the Westminster Greek group was a committee of practicing ministers dedicated to mainstream Christianity. They were churchmen first and scholars second. So they were the most effective modern spokesmen for the great letter writers of the early Christian Church.

THE MISSION PARAMOUNT

There was a uniform brilliance to the decisions that King James and Archbishop Bancroft made in dividing the Bible text among the six committees of scholars. These decisions were sometimes ecumenical, sometimes conservative, sometimes convenient. But they were always practical–and in the best interest of the Biblical material itself.

It's not hard to imagine that–as these Puritans and Arminians and high churchmen met in their committee rooms–there were earnest debates. There may even have been theological explosions. But what must have sustained the translators, during year after year of tedious and exacting labor, was an exalted sense of their mission–to

forge an English Bible that would stand through the centuries, one
that was not only fair to a range of theological concerns but also so
true to the original texts that it would be above challenge, above controversy, above failure. And as these worshipful men worked their
way elbow to elbow through the sacred text, that text must have
given them a sure sense of the *divine* presence working with them and
through them and in them.

CHAPTER TWENTY

Publishing the King James Bible in 1611

L ittle information remains to tell us what actually went on in the translation committee rooms as the fifty-four King James scholars toiled to produce what's since been called "the noblest monument in English prose." But, piecing together the reports we do have, we can begin to answer certain basic questions: How soon after they were appointed did the teams begin their work? How closely did they follow the "Rules" that King James had laid down? How democratic were the translation committees? What was their highest priority—fidelity to the original Hebrew and Greek wording, loyalty to the English Crown and Church, or literary beauty?

TIMETABLE FOR THE TRANSLATION

No one knows precisely when the translators began and ended their work. Some scholars think that the work began shortly after James appointed the translators and issued the "Rules" they were to follow—in July of 1604. Others feel the committees didn't start meeting until 1607, after prolonged research. Some feel the teams worked just two years on the project; others, that they labored for more than six years.

  The broadest hint we have as to the translators' schedule shows up in the preface to the first edition of the 1611 Bible. There, Miles Smith, spokesman for the translators, says the King James scholars took much longer preparing their Bible than had the men who supposedly turned out the Septuagint Greek Old Testament in an astounding seventy-two days. "The worke hath not bene hudled up in 72 dayes," he writes, "but hath cost the workemen . . . the paines of twise seven times seventie two dayes and more."

Psalm 23 from The Holy Bible, King James version, 1611

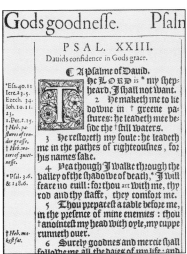

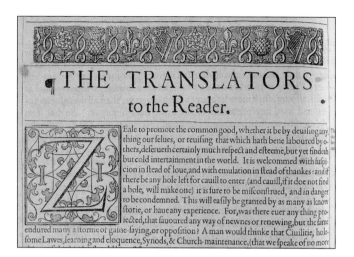

Eale to promote the common good, whether it be by deuifing any
thing our felues, or reuifing that which hath bene laboured by o-
thers, deferueth certainly much refpect and efteeme, but yet findeth
but cold intertainment in the world. It is welcommed with fufpi-
cion in ftead of loue, and with emulation in ftead of thankes : and if
there be any hole left for cauill to enter (and cauill, if it doe not find
a hole, will make one) it is fure to be mifconftrued, and in danger
to be condemned. This will eafily be granted by as many as know
ftorie, or haue any experience. For, was there euer any thing pro-
iected, that fauoured any way of newnes or renewing, but the fame
endured many a ftorme of gaine-faying, or oppofition? A man would thinke that Ciuilitie, hol-
fome Lawes, learning and eloquence, Synods, & Church-maintenance, (that we fpeake of no more

Miles Smith's preface to the
King James Bible

People who take Smith's words literally conclude that the first draft was completed in two years and nine months, or 1,008 days. But there's solid evidence that the translation took much longer than that, especially since Smith also says that the translation was "so long in hand."

One thing seems clear—each committee worked at its own pace. For instance, a letter from the director of the Westminster Hebrew group, Lancelot Andrewes, indicates that his committee was meeting regularly by late 1604. And the Cambridge Hebrew Committee also began its work early, meeting Mondays through Saturdays. Apparently this committee completed its assignment in time for one of its members (the brilliant Greek and Hebrew scholar John Bois) to join the Cambridge Greek Committee for the duration of its work.

Yet the translation as a whole didn't move as quickly as King James thought it should. So, in late 1608, he instructed Archbishop Bancroft to issue a royal order demanding that the Bible be "finished and printed" immediately. But the translators made the king wait for another two and a half years.

SOURCES THE TRANSLATORS USED

A key question for the translators was this: should the new text be a revision of the Bishops' Bible of 1568, as the king's "Rules" dictated, or a fresh translation from the Greek and Hebrew? The king sent forty Bishops' Bibles to the translators—a strong message that they were to stick closely to that text. But Miles Smith indicates this royal directive was largely ignored.

On the one hand, Smith says, "Wee never thought from the beginning, that we should need to make a new Translation . . . but to make a good one better." Yet he also says the translators looked at *all* the previous English Bibles—not just the Bishops' text. They wanted to make "out of many good [Bibles], one principall good one, not justly to be excepted against." So the translators apparently decided to take the best from the previous English Bibles and eliminate the worst—melding the earlier versions together into one supremely beautiful text.

Smith goes on to defend the translators' right to return to the Hebrew and Greek texts also. According to Smith, Hebrew and Greek were the "tongues wherein God was pleased to speake to his Church by his Prophets and Apostles." He says the translators also consulted the Old Chaldaic, Syrian, and Latin texts, as well as numerous modern translations. So Smith's preface dispels any notion that the translators allowed themselves to be strapped to the Bishops' Bible.

HOW THE TRANSLATION WAS ACCOMPLISHED

There were three main steps in the translation process. First, each committee forged a rough draft of the books of the Bible assigned to it. Second, a reviewing committee in London reworked these drafts. Third, Bishop Thomas Bilson of Winchester and Miles Smith of the Oxford Hebrew team gave the whole Bible manuscript a final editing.

The translators worked more or less democratically. They debated verse by verse just how the text should read. Richard Kilbye, a member of the Oxford Hebrew group, once told a young churchman who was critical of a certain wording in the King James Bible that the passage in question had been the object of a heated argument within the committee, and that it had finally been chosen over *thirteen* other possible renderings.

Most of the teams followed James's "Rules." Each translator prepared his own "amended" version of the text assigned to his committee and brought it to the group meetings for discussion. Then the translators would read aloud their proposed wordings as the others offered their comments. Eventually they'd reach a consensus on the passage being reviewed.

Many of the wordings that the committees decided *against* ended up as marginal notes. In fact, the most convincing evidence of how democratically the translators worked is the heavy marginal annotation throughout the original 1611 Bible. Virtually every scholar's opinion found expression in the

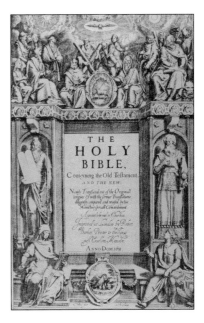

Title page of the 1611 edition of the King James Bible

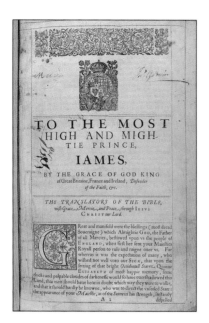

The dedication to
King James

margins. In the Old Testament, there are some sixty-five hundred marginal glosses—more than in any previous Bible. In the New Testament, there are over seven hundred glosses. Miles Smith points out that the variety of marginal glosses gives readers the freedom to choose whatever interpretation they wish.

PRINCIPAL INFLUENCES

At Cambridge and Oxford, trouble erupted soon after the translation began. Committee members started squabbling over the king's "Rules." James responded by appointing a board of overseers at each university to keep the radical translators in line. Although James had initially wanted to please the Anglican Church hierarchy by using the Bishops' Bible as the basis for translation, there's evidence that he actually preferred the radical Protestant texts—especially the Tyndale and Geneva Bibles. So he informally let the translators know that they could use those Bibles in their work.

The translators also felt free to employ the vast array of newly published Bible texts and commentaries available to them. Among the ancient-language texts they used were the Hebrew Masoretic Bible printed in 1494, the Complutensian Polyglot of 1520, the Antwerp Polyglot of Hebrew and Greek texts of 1569–1572, the Greek Septuagint from the third century B.C., Erasmus' Greek text of 1516, and Jerome's Vulgate Bible, as well as virtually every other recently discovered Hebrew, Greek, and Latin Bible text.

In addition, as Smith's preface explains, the King James scholars used nearly every available modern Bible translation—including Luther's Bible. The translators' greatest debt, though, was to the magnificent English Bible tradition—to Tyndale's Bible, Matthew's, Coverdale's, the Great Bible, the Cranmer Bible, the beloved Geneva Bible, and even the Bishops' Bible. Besides those, there were two other versions of the English Bible that the translators leaned on, ones that were almost unmentionable among the Anglican hierarchy—the Catholic Rheims New Testament of 1582 and a Bible by the illustrious but cranky Puritan scholar Hugh Broughton. For years, Broughton had

been lobbying for a new and more accurate Bible translation, and he
eventually produced one of his own, one that reflected not only his
brilliance but also, unfortunately, his bias and intellectual arrogance.

THE REVIEWING BOARD

As James's "Rules" had outlined, the entire manuscript of the new
Bible went to a reviewing board. This board was made up of representatives from each translation location—Oxford, Cambridge, and Westminster. The revisers met every day for approximately nine months,
sometime between 1610 and 1611.

The best account we have of the reviewing board's work is by
one of its members—Hebrew and Greek scholar John Bois. Bois's notes
reveal who some of the other reviewers were: his own mentor, the
famous Hebrew and Greek scholar Andrew Downes; the Calvinist
Greek scholar John Harmer; and probably Arthur Lake, a freethinking
bishop known to his friends as "a living library."

Also, Bois's notes indicate there was plenty of healthy dissent
on the reviewing board. Sometimes the debate centered on a subtle

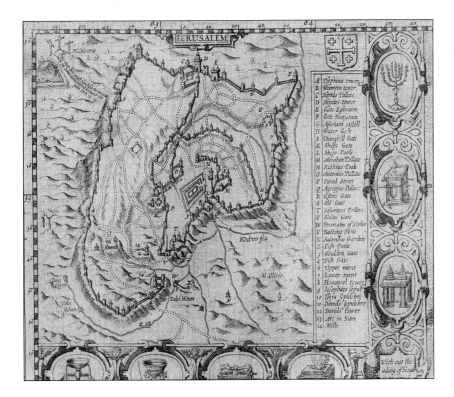

*Portion of a map of Jerusalem
from the 1611 edition of the
King James Bible*

linguistic or theological point. Other times it centered on the place-
ment of a comma (as in their discussion of Romans 11:31). Sometimes
the revisers appear to have been defending James's position as king.
In their translation of I Peter 2:13, for example, they changed the
phrase "the emperor as supreme" to "the king, as supreme."

One thing seems apparent, though—the revisers were *not* the
last ones to edit the King James Bible. The text that Bois gives in his
notes is vastly different from the King James text that was eventually
published. It lacks the poetic phrasing, sonority, and rhythm that make
the King James text so unforgettable.

At most, the reviewing board's work on the King James Bible
shows the text in an intermediate stage. Beyond their London revision
lay a final and crucial level of editing—one that determined the lasting
place the King James Bible holds in the history of English literature.

THE FINAL EDITORS

Two reliable contemporary reports indicate that the key level of review
was done by Bishop Thomas Bilson and Miles Smith. One account
describes the final editing this way: "Bilson, Bishop of Winchester, and
Dr. Myles Smith, who from the beginning had been very active in the
affair, again received the whole work, and prefixed arguments to the
several books; and . . . Dr. Smith, who for his indefatigable pains taken
in this work was soon after the printing of it, deservedly made Bishop
of Gloucester, was ordered to write a preface to it, the same which is
now printed in the folio editions of this Bible."

In both accounts the real emphasis is on *the monumental contri-
bution Miles Smith made to the King James Bible.* As one report says, Smith
"had been deeply occupied in the whole work from the beginning."
Bilson, on the other hand, had not been involved in the translation at
an earlier stage. And, though he was an experienced Bible scholar
and linguist, he was probably appointed more as a representative of
conservative church thinking than for his editing and writing ability.

The preface to Smith's *Sermons,* published in 1632, reveals just
how crucial his role was in the translation. The author of the preface
describes Smith as "a chiefe one" who "began with the first, and was
the last man of the Translators in the worke."

Certainly Smith's own words in the preface to the 1611 Bible show his special fitness to serve as the final and chief editor of the new publication. The preface demonstrates his passionate devotion to the Protestant ideal of putting the Bible in common, everyday language. And it reveals Smith as a self-effacing servant of God, eager to give full credit to his fellow translators as "greater in other mens eyes then in their owne, that sought the truth rather than their own praise."

Most important, the preface shows Smith as a master of the English language—one who wrote simply, grandly, rhythmically, and memorably. Almost every line of the preface echoes the Hebraic rhythms of the King James text. Here's just one example, lifted at random: the Scriptures, Smith says, "can make us wise unto salvation . . . . If we be ignorant, they will instruct us; if out of the way, they wil bring us home; if out of order, they wil reforme us; if in heavines, comfort us; if dul, quicken us; if colde, inflame us."

It was probably Bilson who wrote the fulsome dedication "To the most high and mighty Prince James." (The dedication still appears at the front of the Bible.) And most scholars think Bilson wrote the summaries at the top of each page of the Bible. But it probably fell to both editors to check punctuation, capitalization, and spelling.

Smith and Bilson also (in the words of one report) "maturely weighed and examined" the Bible to make sure it was fair to both the king and the Anglican Church. And since they represented different wings of the Church (Smith was a Calvinist and Bilson a high churchman), the two brought an ideal balance to the final editing process.

Yet it was undoubtedly Miles Smith alone who was responsible for transforming the manuscript into a masterpiece of prose art. He returned again and again to Tyndale's Bible, with its simple, informal word choice and its powerful rhythmic phrasing. He was the great anonymous editor-in-chief who wove together with such felicity all the previous English Bibles.

THE STYLE

Some feel that the triumph of the King James Version is its ecumenicity, its universality. Others, like Bible scholar Craig Thompson, feel that "the supremacy of the King James version is one of style." Yet the translators and editors didn't invent a new style. Their genius lay in smoothing, updating, and streamlining an old style—making it sound more folksy and down-to-earth. And they managed to do this without destroying the vigor and melody of the original Hebraic texts or the cadence and power of the previous English Bibles.

How did the translators do all this? By deciding up front to create a Bible that would be at its best when read aloud. In other words, they wanted a Bible that *sounded* good, one whose phrases were easy to remember and hard to forget. So they set out to piece together a mosaic of past texts—one that would have more melody, majesty, and overall appeal than any earlier English Bible.

PUBLICATION AND AUTHORIZATION

After a quick check-over by Archbishop Bancroft, and perhaps even by King James himself, the new Bible was ready for printing at the press of Robert Barker, the royal printer. Barker produced two lavish editions of the text, both printed in 1611. He used the most expensive rag paper available and an innovative combination of boldface and roman type. And he commissioned new artwork by Cornelius Boel of Antwerp for the title page.

Following that came Bilson's dedication, Smith's preface, a calendar of Anglican feast days, and—among other things—a pictorial Bible genealogy and a map of the Holy Land compiled by the outstanding cartographer of the age, John Speed.

The most significant decision James made concerning the publication of the Bible was to issue it freely in *all sizes*—ranging from the large cathedral edition to a pocket edition for home reading. So, for the first time in English history, the Bible was available at a price *everyone* could afford.

James allowed the phrase "Appointed to be read in Churches" to appear on the title page—a public announcement that this Bible was to replace forever the Bishops' Bible as the authorized English text. For this reason, the King James Bible is often referred to as the Authorized Version.

THE ACHIEVEMENT

"Zeale to promote the common good"–that's the quality that, according to Miles Smith's preface, was the driving force behind the translators' work on the King James Bible. It was this "zeale" that inspired their exhaustive research, their determination to hammer out a truly ecumenical text, and their care in preserving and heightening the beauty of the basic English Bible. The translators knew that their king and Church faced a serious threat from both Roman Catholics and radical Calvinists. And they saw the new Bible as their primary hope of restoring national unity.

King James's translators invested, without any pay, six to eight years of their lives in laboring over a new version of Scripture. This fact alone testifies to the depth of their commitment to the mission and promise of the King James Bible. And the text of the Bible they produced demonstrates that the "zeale" of the king and his scholars was not wasted. They achieved–in their committee rooms and in the pages of their Bible–a national consensus of faith. Theirs was indeed the first version of Scriptures consecrated to the *entire* English populace, for its "common good."

IX
CONCLUSION
AND
UPDATE

CHAPTER TWENTY-ONE

Breaking Barriers to the Bible: From Print to Video to Outer Space

L ighten up!" Could that be what God said when He created the world? And the serpent who tempted Eve—was he "one bad dude"? All this might sound light-years away from the Renaissance English of the King James Bible. And it is. It comes from *The Black Bible Chronicles, Book One: From Genesis to the Promised Land.*

Written in "hip-hop" slang, this Bible is designed to reach young people. Listen to the words of P. K. McCary, a Bible-studies teacher and author of this version of the Bible: "When an 11-year-old girl tells me that the Serpent [in the story of Adam and Eve in the garden of Eden] reminds her of a crack dealer, something great is happening. I want kids to see why God's word is relevant to their lives. I look forward to the day when, on any street corner, they not only talk about the great play Michael Jordan made, but the great plays God has performed for them."

Translations such as this "hip-hop" Bible are among hundreds of versions of the English Scriptures undertaken since the publication of the King James Bible in 1611. Some are considered mainstream. Others are on the fringes. Still others are essentially reworks of the King James text.

REVISIONS OF THE KING JAMES BIBLE

Not long after the publication of the King James Version, minor updates of the original began to appear. In fact, the Bible was updated four times in the first century and a half after its publication—in 1627, 1638, 1762, and 1769.

The King James text has also undergone several major *modern* revisions. The first of these major revisions was published in 1885 as the *English Revised Version.* Its purpose was to keep the language current with the times. Also, the revisers wanted to take advantage of contemporary Bible scholarship.

A number of ancient manuscripts had been discovered that needed to be examined in light of the King James Version. And the revisers wanted to remove what they felt was "medieval mythology" from the King James text. The term *Lucifer,* for example, was changed to *day star* in the Revised Version.

In 1901, a second revision of the King James text came out. Called the *American Standard Version,* it gave a uniquely American sound to the text. The term *Holy Ghost,* for instance, which appeared in the *English Revised Version,* was replaced by *Holy Spirit.*

Still another revision of the King James Bible was published in 1952. Known as the *Revised Standard Version,* it moved away from certain literal and archaic wordings. Also, its translators took into account several twentieth-century archaeological finds, such as the Dead Sea Scrolls. When this version was published, it fueled several Bible burnings. These protests were against the changed wording in Isaiah 7:14, where the word *virgin* was changed to *young woman.* This edition was popular, however. A million copies—the entire first edition—sold in just two days. By 1981, some fifty million copies of the Bible had been sold.

In 1982, another King James revision—called the *New King James Version*—came out. The ecumenical and worldwide group of translators working on this text tried to make it easier to read than previous revisions, but they also stayed very close to the original. Words such as *thee* and *thou* were removed, and quotation marks were inserted to highlight conversations within the text.

The most recent revision of the King James Bible, the *New Revised Standard Version,* was published in 1990. Again, the use of contemporary language was a major concern, as well as the use of such inclusive wording as *humankind* instead of *man* in Genesis 1:26.

THE FIRST MODERN TRANSLATIONS

After it first came out in 1611, the King James Version won the hearts of English-speaking people everywhere. Efforts to displace it failed. The Calvinist Geneva Bible, for instance, was republished a couple of times (in 1613 and 1640), but English-speaking men and women refused to return to its slanted Calvinist wording.

It wasn't until the latter part of the nineteenth century that scholars retranslated the Bible into English from scratch. One of the first of these was an American woman named Julia Smith.

Born into a well-educated Glastonbury, Connecticut, family in the early part of the nineteenth century, Smith had an insatiable thirst for learning. Though not religious in a formal sense, her family was deeply devout and loved the Bible. Smith studied Greek and Latin at the academy in Glastonbury and attended seminary for a year in New York State. But because most colleges wouldn't admit women at that time in the United States, she couldn't continue with a university education. Yet nothing was more important to her than understanding the Bible. And she was sure that the only way to do that was to translate Scripture for herself from the Greek and Hebrew.

In all, Julia Smith translated the Bible five times: twice from the Hebrew, twice from the Greek, and once from Latin. Her final product, the *Julia Smith Bible,* was published in 1876. Smith was also a leader in the antislavery movement and fought for women's rights. She refused to pay taxes until she was given the right to vote.

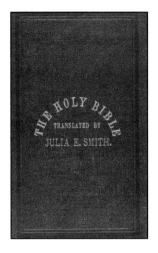

Julia Smith's Bible

EARLY TWENTIETH-CENTURY TRANSLATIONS

One of the first important new Bibles of the century, *The Historical New Testament* by Oxford professor James Moffatt, was published in 1901. In this version, the translator arranged the New Testament in "the order of its literary growth" and "according to the dates of the documents."

Then, in 1903, came Ferrar Fenton's *Holy Bible in Modern English.* Fenton, a British businessman, came up with some fresh wordings— like *Everliving* for the Hebrew *Yahweh.* He also reordered the New Testament, placing the Gospel of John first.

Four volumes of Ferrar Fenton's translation of the Bible

Gerald Warre Cornish was a Cambridge graduate and lecturer in Greek at Manchester University in England when he was called into active service during World War I. He was killed in action in September 1916. Among Cornish's wartime effects, found after his death, was a soiled manuscript of Corinthians and Ephesians. The clear, unusual style of his original translation comes through in this passage from I Corinthians 6: "Now another matter–the Greeks are devoted to litigation, it is a passion with them, but what has that to do with you? Are you going to haunt the law-courts of Corinth with cases which you bring against one another! This has little to do with the true judgement and justice which your faith exemplifies." Cornish's translation, *Saint Paul from the Trenches,* was published posthumously in 1937.

The first Old Testament translation by Jewish scholars appeared in 1917. Called *The Holy Scriptures According to the Masoretic Text, a New Translation,* the books are put together in the same order as in the Hebrew Bible.

In 1924, another woman Bible translator–Helen B. Montgomery–turned out *The Centenary Translation of the New Testament.* This Bible was intended to celebrate the one hundred years of Bible distribution by the American Baptist Publication Society. Montgomery, a graduate of Wellesley College, was a Baptist minister as well as a good friend of women's rights advocate Susan B. Anthony.

Montgomery wanted to stay close to the "beloved" King James text but at the same time to produce a Bible that was worded in ordinary spoken English. She published her Bible in a size that would fit easily in a handbag.

In 1926, James Moffatt published his second Bible–this one a complete version, commonly known as "the Moffatt Bible." A professor of Greek and New Testament at Union Theological Seminary in New York, Moffatt felt that "the ideal of the translator is to let his readers enjoy part of that pleasure which the original once afforded to its audience in some far-off century." Putting this theory into practice, he came up with some radically new wordings—like *sheiks* for *elders,* the *Eternal* for *God,* and *barge* for Noah's *ark.*

Another prominent version of Scripture, *The Complete Bible: An American Translation,* came out in its original form in 1931. Known as the "Chicago Bible," this translation was done by a group of professors at the University of Chicago. Their aim was to produce a Bible in the idiom of everyday American life. So they eliminated archaic expressions like *doest* and *makest* from the text and converted words like *thou* to *you.*

British and American translators who put out *The Westminster Version of the Sacred Scriptures* in 1935 had a similar aim. They felt strongly that "intelligibility" should be "the first requisite in any translation" and that "no considerations of beauty or dignity" should be as important as clarity. This Bible had been commissioned some eighty years earlier by Westminster Church officials in England. The translators drew heavily on Jerome's Latin Vulgate as source material.

8 heard if they use words enough. You must not be like them. For
9 who is your Father, knows what you need before you ask him;
therefore, is the way you are to pray:
  'Our Father in heaven,
  Your name be revered!
10 Your kingdom come!
  Your will be done on earth as it is done in heaven!
11 Give us today bread for the day,
12 And forgive us our debts, as we have forgiven our debtors,
13 And do not subject us to temptation,
  But save us from the evil one.'
14 For if you forgive others when they offend you, your heavenly
15 will forgive you too. But if you do not forgive others when the

The Lord's Prayer in the "Chicago Bible"

MID-TWENTIETH-CENTURY BIBLES

Take an eight-hundred-and-fifty-word vocabulary, add fifty Biblical terms and one hundred words that help glue verses together, and you have the easy-to-understand contents of *The Basic Bible in English,* published in 1949. This Bible, put out by Cambridge University Press, limits its overall vocabulary to a mere one thousand words. It was translated by scholars at the University of London.

Charles Kingsley Williams of England, another vocabulary-conscious Bible translator, was for many years a missionary and teacher in India and Africa. Many people in these cultures were confused by the King James prose, so he often translated Bible passages for them directly from the Greek.

When he retired in England, Williams spent fifteen years weaving bits and pieces of his translation into *The New Testament, A New Translation in Plain English,* published in 1952. Williams kept his translation to about fifteen hundred common English words, plus some one hundred and sixty doctrinal terms.

Unlike Williams, Kenneth Wuest–a teacher of Greek at the Moody Bible Institute in Chicago–was *not* an advocate of limited-vocabulary Bible translation. Instead, Wuest's aim was to shed what he called the "linguistic strait-jacket" of previous Bibles and produce an "expanded version" that used as many words as he felt were needed in order to convey Bible truth. Wuest's *Expanded Translation of the Greek New Testament* was published in 1956.

Two years later, J. B. Phillips published his *New Testament in Modern English*. Phillips had been a vicar in a parish church in England during World War II. Feeling that his parish faced great danger–much as the early Christians had–he wanted to give his congregation, especially the youth group, a reading of the Scriptures that would be not quite as formal as the King James Version but would offer them encouragement in language that they could easily understand. So, while the bombs fell on London, Phillips launched into a contemporary English translation of the Bible. Encouraged by the Christian writer C. S. Lewis, Phillips published his New Testament bit by bit. It was enormously popular.

Calling on Cub Scouts and school-age children for assistance, Jay P. Green published *The Children's Version of the Holy Bible* in 1960. Green had the children underline all the words in the Authorized Version that they couldn't understand. Then he replaced these with words that they could understand but that would stay true to the original. His Bible is printed in large typeface, and the text is written in paragraphs rather than in verses.

The Jerusalem Bible (1966) is the English translation of *La Bible de Jérusalem*, a French Bible put out by the Dominican Biblical School in Jerusalem. This Bible was the first complete Roman Catholic version to be translated from the original Hebrew and Greek. The English text was prepared by twenty members of the British Catholic Biblical Association, including J. R. R. Tolkien, author of *Lord of the Rings*.

A revision of this Bible, *The New Jerusalem Bible*, was published in 1985. This rendition uses "inclusive" language in terms of gender. For example, the verse in Psalms that in the King James Version reads "Happy is the man" is reworded as "How blessed is anyone."

Throughout the 1960s, a Protestant translation team was busy in England putting together another Bible in modern English—one that would *not* be based on Tyndale's wording. The Bible they produced, *The New English Bible,* targets young readers and people interested in private Bible study—rather than church congregations. This version, originally published in 1970, was republished in 1989 as *The Revised English Bible.*

A meeting of the Joint Committee of sponsoring churches working toward publication of the complete New English Bible

RECENT BIBLES: REACHING SPECIAL READERS

A Bible translation that some have considered one of the greatest success stories in the history of publishing—*The Living Bible, Paraphrased*—arrived in bookstores in 1971. This Bible is the work of one man, Kenneth Taylor, who was intrigued by the concept of a "thought-for-thought" translation. Believing that most Bibles are theologically biased, Taylor wanted to be honest enough to state his theological stance up front—a stance that is, in his case, a "rigid evangelical position." During the 1970s, this translation captured 46 percent of Bible sales in the United States and was translated into some one hundred of the world's languages.

Another new Bible with a distinctive flavor is Clarence Jordan's *The Cotton Patch Version of Hebrew and General Epistles* (1973). The translator calls his Bible "a modern translation in a Southern accent." A resident of the American South, Jordan was an agriculturalist and a civil rights advocate with a Ph.D. in New Testament Greek. Instead of the word *crucifixion,* Jordan uses the word *lynching.* And he calls Paul's letter to the Philippians "The Letter to the Alabaster African Church, Smithville, Alabama."

The Good News Bible is an attempt by Bible Societies worldwide to publish a Bible in English for everyone who either is a native English speaker or uses English as a second language. English words that aren't used in everyday speech have been eliminated from this easy-to-read translation, published in 1976.

Stack of assorted translations of the Bible

The *Contemporary English Version,* or CEV, is a new Bible being produced by the American Bible Society. The entire Bible, translated directly from the Hebrew and Greek, was published in 1995. At first, this version was geared toward youngsters. But the clear and simple language of the translation, which stays very close to the original text, was such a hit with adults that the Bible Society decided to promote it for *all* English-speaking readers.

Fans of the popular television series *Star Trek* may be pleased to know that consideration is being given to translating the Bible into Klingon—the make-believe language of the caveman-like aliens in the series. At the first meeting of the Klingon Language Institute in Philadelphia, in July 1994, the group commissioned a special Klingon Bible translation.

According to the group's founder, Professor Lawrence Shoen, the experiment goes beyond fun. He feels the project will help group members when "it comes to learning another terrestrial language." The Klingon language was concocted from dialects of the Pacific Northwest Native American tribes—as well as a combination of Japanese, English, and German sounds.

Creole-speaking West Indians also have a new Bible translation written in Jamaican patois—the Creole dialect spoken in many parts of the Caribbean. This translation, undertaken by the United Bible Society and Jamaican religious leaders, lends new credibility to the West Indian Creole language. The Bible targets "the unchurched and people living in ghetto areas."

ELECTRONIC VERSIONS OF THE BIBLE

The American Bible Society is sponsoring a multimillion-dollar project to produce a rock video "translation" of the Bible. This version, designed especially for young people, will feature some ten or twelve Bible stories interpreted from a late-twentieth-century standpoint. The first segment of the series—a blaring but moving rendition of Jesus' healing of the Gadarene demoniac—pictures Jesus as a jeans-clad welder and the demoniac as an inner-city drug addict.

Also in progress is a thirty-hour television rendering of the Old Testament. The first segment of this series was aired in 1994 in the United States and focuses on the life of Abraham. Actor Richard Harris plays the lead role in the segment on Abraham, which was filmed in the southern Moroccan desert. Harris says Abraham changed his life. "It's been a terrific spiritual influence," he says, "very deep and very moving."

THE UNIVERSALITY OF SCRIPTURAL TEXTS

Some contemporary variations of the Gospels have been produced by people "outside" traditional Christianity. Stephen Mitchell, for instance, has published *The Gospel According to Jesus.* Mitchell, a Zen Buddhist and a translator of ancient Chinese Scripture, sees what he considers a great compatibility between the teachings of Jesus and those of other religions. He says, "Jesus speaks in harmony with the supreme teachings of all the great religions: the Upanishads, the Tao Te Ching, the Buddhist sutras, the Zen and Sufi and Hasidic Masters." Mitchell observes that "when the words arise from the deepest kind of spiritual experience, from a heart pure of doctrines and beliefs, they transcend religious boundaries, and can speak to all people, male and female, bond and free, Greek and Jew." It's these universal aspects of Scripture that he brings out in what he calls his "essential" version of the gospel story.

The Bible translation movement has accelerated explosively since the early 1800s, thanks in large part to the international Bible Society movement that was born at that time. In 1800, the complete Bible was available in fewer than fifty languages. Now it's available in three hundred and thirty-three. Then you could read portions of the Bible in just sixty-eight languages; now you can read Bible portions in a staggering two thousand and eighteen. These translations span nearly every continent and touch most every earthly culture and language—from Akhoe in Namibia to Zuni in New Mexico. And Bible Societies continue to fill in the gaps.

So the Bible is, in a sense, uniting the world in a universal language of Scripture—a universal language of divine Love. Together, the many versions of Scripture today represent the multifarious ways that the Word of divinity is reaching all men, women, and children— healing, regenerating, and reforming them.

Selected Bibliography

Abbot, George. *A Brief Description of the Whole Worlde*. London, 1656; facsimile ed., New York: Da Capo Press, 1970.

Anderson, Bernhard. *Understanding the Old Testament,* 4th ed. Englewood Cliffs, N.J.: Prentice-Hall, 1986.

Andrewes, Lancelot. *Private Devotions of Lancelot Andrewes*. Edited by F. E. Brightman. Magnolia, Mass.: Peter Smith, 1961.

———. *The works of Lancelot Andrewes, sometime bishop of Winchester.* Oxford: J. H. Parker, 1841–1854; reprint ed., New York: AMS Press, 1967.

Attwater, Donald. *The Penguin Dictionary of Saints*. Harmondsworth: Penguin, 1975.

Bacon, Francis. *The Works of Francis Bacon*. Edited by James Spedding, Robert Leslie Ellis, and Douglas Denon Heath. 10 vols. London: Longham, 1857–1874; reprint ed., New York: Garrett Press, 1968.

Bainton, Roland H. *The Reformation of the Sixteenth Century*. Boston: Beacon Press, 1985.

Bancroft, Richard. *Dangerous positions and proceedings . . .* London: J. Wolfe, 1593; facsimile ed., New York: Da Capo Press, 1972.

Barlow, William. *An Answer to a Catholike English-man . . .* London: Mathew Law, 1609.

Belloc, Hilaire. *Cranmer, Archbishop of Canterbury, 1533–1556*. Philadelphia: J. B. Lippincott, 1931.

Berry, Lloyd E., gen. ed. *The Bible and Holy Scriptures Conteyned in the Olde and Newe Testament. Translated according to the Ebrue and Greke, and conferred with the best translations in divers langages.* Geneva: Rouland Hall, 1560; facsimile ed., Madison: University of Wisconsin Press, 1969.

Biblia Sacra Iuxta Vulgatam Clementinam Nova Editio, 4th ed. Edited by Alberto Colunga and Laurentio Turrado. Madrid: Biblioteca de Autores Cristianos, 1965.

Bilson, Thomas. *The True Difference Betweene Christian Subiection and Unchristian Rebellion . . .* Oxford: Ioseph Barnes, 1585; reprint ed., New York: Da Capo Press, 1972.

Bois, John. *The Workes of John Boys, Doctor in Divinitie and Deane of Canterburie.* London: John Haviland for William Aspley, 1622.

The Booke of Common Prayer, and Administration of the sacraments, And other Rites and Ceremonies of the Church of England. London: Robert Barker, 1605. Bound with *The Bible, That is, The Holy Scriptures Contained in the Old and New Testament.* London: Robert Barer, 1602.

Brasenose College Register, 1509–1909. Oxford: Blackwell, 1909. S.v. "Savile, Henry."

Brett, Richard. *Iconum Sacrarum Decas . . .* Oxford: Joseph Barnes, 1603.

British Museum General Catalogue of Printed Books. London: Balding-Mansell, 1965. S.v. "Bible."

Broughton, Hugh. *Master Broughton's Letters . . .* London: John Wolfe, 1599.

Bruce, F. F. *The English Bible: A History of Translations.* New York: Oxford University Press, 1961.

———. *History of the Bible in English.* New York: Oxford University Press, 1978.

Butterworth, Charles C. *The Literary Lineage of the King James Bible, 1340–1611.* Philadelphia: University of Pennsylvania Press, 1941.

Cambridge History of the English Bible. Vols. 1–3. Cambridge: University Press, 1980.

Campbell, Joseph. *Primitive Mythology: The Masks of God.* Harmondsworth: Penguin, 1987.

Cardwell, Edward. *Synodalia: A Collection of Articles of Religion, Canons, and Proceedings of Convocations in the Province of Canterbury, From the Year 1574 To the Year 1717.* 4 vols. Reprint ed., Oxford: University Press, 1942.

Catholic Encyclopedia. 1967 ed. S.v. "Vulgate," by L. F. Hartman.

Chaderton, Laurence. *An Excellent and Godly Sermon . . .* London: Christopher Barker, 1580.

Chadwick, Henry. *The Early Church.* Harmondsworth: Penguin, 1967.

Chamberlain, John. *The Chamberlain Letters; A Selection of the Letters of John Chamberlain Concerning Life in England from 1597 to 1626.* Edited by Elizabeth McClure Thomson. New York: G. P. Putnam, 1965.

Chase, Mary Ellen. *The Bible and the Common Reader.* New York: Macmillan, 1945.

Christian History. Issue 34, Vol. 11, No. 2.

——. Issue 39, Vol. 12, No. 3.

Conant, Hannah O'Brien (Chaplin). *The English Bible.* New York: Sheldon, Blakeman, 1856.

Cooper, Charles Henry. *Athenae Cantabrigienses.* 2 vols. Farnborough, Hants: Gregg International.

Cooper, Lane. *Certain Rhythms in the English Bible.* Ithaca: Cornell University Press, 1952.

Coverdale's Byble. Zurich: Christopher Froschover, 1550.

Cowie, Leonard. *Martin Luther, Leader of the Reformation.* New York: Praeger, 1969.

——. *The Reformation.* New York: John Day, 1968.

Cranmer, Thomas. *The Works of Thomas Cranmer, Archbishop of Canterbury, Martyr, 1556.* Edited by John Edmund Cox, Parker Society. Cambridge: University Press, 1846.

Daiches, David. *The King James Version of the English Bible.* Chicago: University of Chicago Press, 1941.

Dictionary of National Biography, 1967–1968 ed. Passim.

Dillingham, Francis. *A Dissuasive From Poperie . . .* Cambridge: Iohn Legat, 1599.

Dillingham, William. *Laurence Chaderton, D. D.* Translated by Evelyn Shirley Shuckburgh. Cambridge: MacMillan and Bowes, 1884.

Downes, Andrew. *Eratosthenes, hoc est . . .* Cambridge: John Legate, 1543.

Eedes, Richard. *Six Learned and godly Sermons: Preached some of them before the Kings Maiestie, some before Queene Elizabeth.* London: Edward Bishop, 1604.

The English Hexapla. London: Samuel Bagster and Sons, n.d.

Featley, Daniel. *The Dippers Dipt. or the Anabaptists Duck'd and Plung'd Over Head and Eares, at a Disputation in Southwark.* London: Nicholas Bourne, 1645.

———. *The Grand Sacrilege of the Church of Rome . . .* London: Robert Milbourne, 1630.

———. *A Parallel of new-old Pelagiarminian error.* London: Robert Milbourne, 1626.

Fenton, Roger. *A Sermon Preached at Mercers chappell in Lent 1614.* London: William Aspley, 1616.

Foxe, John. *Actes and Monuments . . .* 8 vols. London: Iohn Day, n.a.; facsimile ed., New York: AMS Press, 1965.

———. *Book of Martyrs . . .* New York: Worthington, 1888.

Froude, James Anthony. *Lectures on the Council of Trent, delivered at Oxford 1892–3.* New York: Charles Scribner, 1896.

Fulke, William. *A Defence of the sincere and true Translations of the holie Scriptures into the English tong.* Edited by Charles Henry Hartshorne. London: Henrie Bynneman, 1583; reprint ed., Cambridge: University Press, 1843.

Fuller, Thomas. *Abel Redivivus: or the dead yet speaking. The lives and Deaths of the Moderne Divines.* London: Thomas Brudenell for John Stafford, 1651.

———. *The Worthies of England.* Edited by John Freeman. London: Allen & Unwin, 1952.

Goodspeed, Edgar J. *The Making of the English New Testament.* Chicago: University of Chicago Press, 1925.

Gray, Arthur. *Cambridge and Its Story.* London: Mathuen, 1912.

Grierson, Sir Herbert. *The English Bible.* London: Collins, 1944.

Harper's Bible Commentary. Edited by James L. Mays. New York: Harper, 1988.

Harrison, G. B. *A Second Jacobean Journal: Being a record of Those Things Most Talked of during the Years 1607 to 1610.* Ann Arbor: University of Michigan Press, 1958.

Herbert, Arthur Sumner, ed. *Historical Catalogue of printed editions of the English Bible: 1525–1961; revised and expanded from the edition of T. H. Darlow and H. F. Moule, 1903.* New York: American Bible Society, 1968.

Hiers, Richard H. *Reading the Bible Book by Book.* Philadelphia: Fortress Press, 1988.

Hillerbrand, Hans J. *The World of the Reformation.* New York: Charles Scribner, 1973.

The Holie Bible Faithfully Translated into English, out of the Authentical Latin. Diligently conferred with the Hebrew, Greek, and other Editions in divers languages. Doway: Laurence Kellam, 1609.

Holinshed, Raphael. *Holinshed's Chronicles: England, Scotland, and Ireland.* 6 vols. London: J. Johnson, 1807; reprint ed., New York: AMS Press, 1965.

Holland, Thomas. *D. Elizabethae Dei gratiâ Angliae, Franciae, & Hiberniae Reginae. A Sermon Preached at Pauls in London the 17. of November Ann. Dom., 1599 . . .* Oxford: Joseph Barnes, 1601.

The Holy Scriptures According to the Masoretic Text. Philadelphia: Jewish Publication Society of America, 1955.

The Interpreter's One-Volume Commentary on the Bible. Edited by Charles M. Laymon. Nashville: Abingdon, 1971.

James I. *Correspondence of King James VI of Scotland with Sir Robert Cecil and Others in England, during the Reign of Queen Elizabeth; with an appendix containing papers illustrative of translations between King James and Robert Earl of Essex.* Edited by John Bruce. Westminster: Camden Soc., 1861.

———. *Letters to Qu. Elizabeth.* London: Camden Soc., 1849.

———. *New Poems by James I of England from a Hitherto Unpublished Manuscript (Add. 24195) in the British Museum.* Edited by Allan F. Westcott. New York: Columbia University Press, 1911.

James I. *The Political Works of James I, Reprinted from the Edition 1616.* Edited by Charles Howard McIlwain. Cambridge, Mass.: Harvard University Press, 1918.

James, Montague R. *The Apocryphal New Testament.* Oxford: Clarendon Press, 1950.

Jedin, Hubert. *A History of the Council of Trent. Translated from the German by Ernest Graf.* 2 vols. London: T. Nelson, 1957.

Jerome, Saint. *The First Desert Hero: Vita Pauli.* Mount Vernon, N.Y.: King Lithographers, 1968.

——. *Select Letters of St. Jerome.* Cambridge, Mass.: Harvard University Press, 1975.

——, comp. *The Histories of the Monks who lived in the Desert of Egypt.* London: n.p., 1904.

Joffe, Linda. "Out of the Desert Comes 'Abraham,'" in *The Christian Science Monitor,* March 22, 1994.

Kee, Howard Clark. *Understanding the New Testament.* 5th ed. Englewood Cliffs, N.J.: Prentice Hall, 1993.

Kelly, J. N. D. *Jerome: His Life, Writings, and Controversies.* New York: Harper, 1975.

Kilbye, Richard. *The Burthen of a loaden conscience: or the miserie of sinne: set forth by the confession of a miserable sinner.* Cambridge: Cantrell Legge, 1608.

The Koran. Translated by N. J. Dawood. Harmondsworth: Penguin, 1990.

Law, Ernest. *A Short History of Hampton Court.* London: G. Bell, 1926.

L'Estrange, Hammond. *George Abbot, the Unwanted Archbishop, 1562–1633.* Naperville, Ill.: Allenson, 1962.

Lowes, John Livingston. "The Noblest Monument in English Prose," in *Essays in Appreciation.* Boston: Houghton Mifflin, 1936.

Luther, Martin. *Luther's Works.* 54 vols. Edited by E. Theodore Bachmann. Philadelphia: Muhlenberg Press, 1960.

McElwee, William Lloyd. *The Wisest Fool in Christendom; the Reign of King James I and VI.* Westport, Conn.: Greenwood Press, 1958.

May, Herbert G. *Our English Bible in the Making: The Word of Life in Living Language.* Philadelphia: Westminster Press, 1952.

Mitchell, Stephen, trans. *The Gospel According to Jesus.* New York: Harper Perennial, 1993.

Mullinger, James Bass. *The University of Cambridge.* 3 vols. Cambridge: University Press, 1884.

Nichols, John. *The Progresses, Processions, and Magnificent Festivities of King James the First, His Royal Consort, Family and Court.* 2 vols. London: n.p., 1828; reprint ed., New York: B. Franklin, 1967.

Opfell, Olga S. *The King James Bible Translators.* Jefferson, N.C.: McFarland, 1982.

The Oxford Dictionary of the Christian Church. Edited by F. L. Cross. Oxford: University Press, 1990.

Paine, Gustavus S. *The Learned Men.* New York: Thomas Y. Crowell, 1959.

Pollard, Alfred W., ed. *The Holy Bible: A Facsimile in a reduced size of the Authorized Version published in the year 1611.* Oxford: University Press, 1911.

——. *Records of the English Bible.* Oxford: University Press, 1911; reprint ed., Folkestone: William Dawson, 1974.

Pollard, A. W., and G. R. Redgrave. *A Short-Title Catalogue of Books Printed in England, Scotland, & Ireland and of English Books Printed Abroad: 1475–1640.* London: Bibliographical Soc., 1946.

Porter, H. C. *Reformation and Reaction in Tudor Cambridge.* Cambridge: University Press, 1958.

Prior, Thomas. *A Sermon at the Funerall of the Right Reverend Father in God, Miles, Late Lord Bishop of Gloucester: Preached in the Cathedrall Church of Gloucester, upon the ninth of November, 1624.* London: Robert Allot, 1632.

Rainolds, John. *A Defence of the Iudgment of the Reformed Churches . . .* n.p.: 1609.

——. *The Discovery of the Man of Sinne: Wherein is set Forth the changes of Gods Church.* Oxford: Ioseph Barnes, 1614.

Religion and Man. Edited by W. Richard Comstock. New York: Harper, 1971.

Ridley, Jasper. *Thomas Cranmer.* Oxford: Clarendon Press, 1967.

Robinson, H. Wheeler. *The Bible in Its Ancient and English Versions.* Oxford: Clarendon Press, 1940.

Rost, Leonhard. *Judaism Outside the Hebrew Canon.* Nashville: Abingdon, 1976.

Saravia, Hadrian. *Clavi Trabales; or Nailes Fastned by some Great Masters of Assemblyes Confirming the Kings Supremacy. Church Government by Bishops.* London: R. Hodgkinson, 1661.

Savile, Henry. *The Ende of Nero and Beginning of Galba; Fower Bookes of the Histories of Cornelius Tacitus; the Life of Agricola.* Oxford: Joseph Barnes, 1591.

Schwarz, Werner. *Principles and Problems of Biblical Translation: Some Reformation Controversies and Their Background.* Cambridge: University Press, 1955.

Scriptures of the World. Reading, Eng.: United Bible Societies, 1992.

Selden, John. *Table-Talk.* London: 1689; reprint ed., Westminster: A Constable, 1895.

The Septuagint Bible. Translated by Charles Thomson. Edited by C. A. Muses. Indian Hills, Colo.: Falcon's Wing Press, 1954.

Smith, Alan G. R., ed. *The Reign of James VI and I.* New York: St. Martin's Press, 1973.

Smith, Julia, trans. *The Holy Bible.* Hartford: American Publishing, 1876.

Smith, Miles. *Sermons of the Right Reverend Father in God Miles Smith, Late Bishop of Glocester. Transcribed out of His originall Manuscripts and now published for the Common Good.* London: Robert Allot, 1632.

Southern, R. W. *Western Society and the Church in the Middle Ages.* Harmondsworth: Penguin, 1990.

Spencer, John. Preface to Richard Hooker. *Lawes of Ecclesiastical Politie.* London: William Stansby, 1611.

Strype, John. *Annals of the Reformation and Establishment of Religion and other Various Occurrences in the Church of England during Queen Elizabeth's Happy Reign.* 4 vols. Oxford: Clarendon Press, 1824; reprint ed., New York: Burt Franklin, n.d.

Tao Te Ching. Translated by Stephen Mitchell. New York: Harper Perennial, 1988.

Teale, William H. *Lives of English Divines.* London: Joseph Masters, 1846.

Thompson, Craig R. *The Bible in English: 1525–1611.* Washington: Folger Shakespeare Library, 1958.

Thorne, William. *A Kenning-Glasse for a Christian King.* London: J. Harrison, 1603.

Trammell, Mary M. "The Background of the King James Translation." Ph.D. diss., University of Miami, 1978.

Trevelyan, G. M. *Trinity College: An Historical Sketch.* Cambridge: University Press, 1972.

Trustees of the British Museum. *Guide to Manuscripts and Printed Books Exhibited in Celebration of the Tercentenary [of the King James Bible].* London: Oxford University Press, 1911.

Venn, John, and John Archibald Venn. *Alumni Cantabrigienses.* 1922.

Walden, Wayne. *Guidebook to Bible Translations, revised.* Boston: Livingworks, 1991.

Walker, Anthony. *Life of John Bois. In Translating for King James.* Edited by Ward Allen. Nashville: Vanderbilt University Press, 1969.

Ward, Samuel. *Two Elizabethan Puritan Diaries.* Edited by M. M. Knappen. Gloucester, Mass.: Peter Smith, 1966.

Weigle, Luther A., gen. ed. *The New Testament Octapla: Eight English Versions of the New Testament in the Tyndale-King James Tradition.* New York: Thomas Nelson, 1962.

Whitgift, John. *The Works of John Whitgift, D.D. . . .* Edited by John Ayre. 3 vols. Cambridge: University Press, 1853.

Williams, Neville. *The Cardinal and the Secretary.* New York: Macmillan, 1976.

Willoughby, Edwin Eliott. *The Making of the King James Bible; A Monograph.* Los Angeles: Dawson's Book Shop at Plantin Press, 1956.

Wood, Anthony à. *Athenae Oxonienses* . . . London: n.p., 1813; reprint ed., New York: Burt Franklin, 1967.

——. *The History and Antiquities of the Colleges and Halls in the University of Oxford.* Edited by John Gutch. 4 vols. Oxford: Clarendon Press, 1786.

Note: The authors' research also included examination of several hundred original manuscripts at Cambridge and Oxford universities, the British Library, and numerous church and cathedral libraries in England, Scotland, and the United States.

About the Authors

Mary M. Trammell grew up in both Louisville and Boston in a family that loved the Bible and talked about it frequently. At Smith College she did her first course work in Bible history, graduating in 1963.

Research for *The Reforming Power of the Scriptures* began in graduate school at the University of Miami, Florida. There, specializing in Renaissance literature, she wrote both her master's thesis and doctoral dissertation on the King James Bible—its background, its literary quality, its role in the Protestant Reformation, and its enormous impact on subsequent English literature. Her research included study in Britain, where she examined manuscripts and books relating to the publication of the great Bibles of the Reformation—at Oxford and Cambridge universities and the British Library, as well as church and cathedral libraries throughout England and Scotland.

It was at the University of Miami that Dr. Trammell met the minister-turned-academic, Dr. John Isaac McCollum, Jr., who became her dissertation director. From his love of the Scriptures, as passionate as any of the reformers about whom this book is written, she learned the deepest reverence for the Bible.

There followed ten years of teaching at the University of Miami and Florida Atlantic University. While teaching brought the joy of helping students find their talents and potential in literature and writing, Dr. Trammell wanted to help people in a more spiritual way. As she says, "I wanted to help them find God and their real identity as the children of God." This turned her to a new career as a Christian Science practitioner and, later, an authorized teacher.

In 1991 she accepted the position of manager of the Church History Department of The First Church of Christ, Scientist, in Boston. It was during her tenure that the church collection of some 400 rare Bibles, including a first edition of the King James Bible of 1611, was opened to the public for the first time.

In 1992 Dr. Trammell was named associate editor of the Christian Science magazines, the position she continues to hold.

William Dawley, a native of Rhode Island, holds a B.A. degree from the University of Massachusetts and graduated from the Leland Powers School of Radio, Television, and Theater. His career includes work on the staff of *The Christian Science Monitor* and as a news broadcaster with the shortwave service of the same paper. He was assistant manager of the Church History Department of The First Church of Christ, Scientist, and was feature editor of the church magazines. At present he is managing editor of *The Herald of Christian Science,* which is circulated throughout the world in twelve languages.

Mr. Dawley's journalistic experience and research of various religions and Scriptures of the world, including Eastern thought, brought to the writing the insight that the stories of the great reformers of Bible translation were "news"—events to be reported with the immediacy of a breaking story.

Picture Credits

68   *Title page taken from a Hebrew-Latin Bible (1546)*; Church History Department–Sylvester

68   *Partial list of Apocryphal writings from The Holie Bible, Bishops' Bible (1572)*; Church History Department–Sylvester

69   *"An angel guideth Tobit" (1712)*; Church History Department–Sylvester

72   *Title page of New Testament, Coverdale Bible (1535)*; Church History Department–Sylvester

74   *"An angel guideth Tobit" (1712)*; Church History Department–Sylvester

76   *Eighteenth-century print of Alexandria*; Collection of Gay Matthaei

79   *Page from the Apocrypha (1611)*; Church History Department–Sylvester

80   *Olive Tree*; Jewel Grutman

81   *Illustration from Susanna and the judges (1712)*; Church History Department–Sylvester

82   *Illustration from Susanna and the judges (1712)*; Church History Department–Sylvester

84   *Illustration of Judas Maccabaeus (1712)*; Church History Department–Sylvester

85   *Illustration of Bel and the Dragon (1816)*; Church History Department–Sylvester

85   *Illustration of Judith (1816)*; Church History Department–Sylvester

94   *Mainz Psalter*; Jacoby/PRD-HICOG

96   *Illustration of Judas Maccabaeus (1712)*; Church History Department–Sylvester

99   *From the Greek New Testament*; Church History Department–Sylvester

102   *Spine of The Greek New Testament*; Church History Department–Sylvester

104   *Paul healing the lame man at Lystra*; Church History Department–Sylvester

108   *King Charlemagne*; courtesy, the Art Store, Boston, MA

110   *Illuminated page from the Tickhill Psalter*; New York Public Library

111   *Mainz Psalter*; Jacoby/PRD-HICOG

114   *Church at Lutterworth*; Gay Matthaei

116   *Peter being delivered from prison (1824 English Bible)*; Church History Department–Sylvester

117   *Portrait of John Wycliffe*; Art Resource

118   *Oxford University*; Gay Matthaei

119   *Oxford University Chapel*; Gay Matthaei

124   *Wycliffe's New Testament (1848)*; Church History Department–Sylvester

125   *Church at Lutterworth*; Gay Matthaei

128   *"An angel guideth Tobit" (1712)*; Church History Department–Sylvester

129   *The Huss homestead*; Jewel Grutman

130   *Huss's Study*; Gay Matthaei

130   *Bethlehem Chapel, Prague*; Jewel Grutman

131   *Statue of John Huss in Husinec, Bohemia*; Gay Matthaei

132   *The river Swift*; Jewel Grutman

134   *Cover Detail of Rheims-Douai Bible (1875)*; Church History Department–Sylvester

136   *Illustration from Susanna and the judges (1712)*; Church History Department–Sylvester

139   *Martin Luther fixing his theses to the door*; painting by Hugo Vogel

141   *Luther's German Bible (1729)*; Church History Department–Sylvester

142   *Luther's Family*; Church History Department–Sylvester

143   *Luther's Bible (1708)*; Church History Department–Sylvester

144   *Statue of Martin Luther in Worms, Germany*; Mike Mazzaschi/Stock Boston

146   *Illustration of Judas Maccabaeus (1712)*; Church History Department–Sylvester

148   *Tyndale translating the Bible*; painting by W. Johnstone

150   *Tyndale's New Testament (1550)*; Church History Department–Sylvester

151   *Page from facsimile of Tyndale's Bible (1862)*; Church History Department–Sylvester
152   *Title page from Matthew's Bible (1537)*; Church History Department–Sylvester
153   *Matthew's Bible (1537)*; Church History Department–Sylvester
153   *Great Bible (1539)*; Michael D. Sylvester
154   *Fourth edition of Tyndale's Bible (1550)*; Church History Department–Sylvester
156   *Paul healing the lame man at Lystra*; Church History Department–Sylvester
159   *Map from Geneva Bible (1560)*; Church History Department–Sylvester
162   *Title page of the Geneva Bible*; Church History Department–Sylvester
164   *Peter being delivered from prison (1824 English Bible)*; Church History Department–Sylvester
167   *Detail of a page from the Bishops' Bible*; Church History Department–Sylvester
168   *Spine of the Bishops' Bible*; Church History Department–Sylvester
169   *Cover of first edition Bishops' Bible (1568)*; Church History Department–Sylvester
169   *Title page of the Bishops' Bible*; Church History Department–Sylvester
170   *Cover detail of Rheims-Douai Bible (1875)*; Church History Department–Sylvester
174   *Title page of King James Bible (1611)*; Church History Department–Sylvester
176   *"An angel guideth Tobit" (1712)*; Church History Department–Sylvester
178   *King James I of England*; Art Resource/NY
181   *Hampton Court Palace*; Herbert Felton
183   *King James version of Psalms*; Church History Department–Sylvester
184   *Title page of New Testament from first edition King James Bible (1611)*; Church History Department–Sylvester
184   *Detail from King James Bible (1611)*; Church History Department–Sylvester
186   *Illustration from Susanna and the judges (1712)*; Church History Department–Sylvester
192   *West front of Westminster Abbey*; R. Norman Matheny
193   *St. John's College, Cambridge University*; David Mansell
194   *Christ Church College, Oxford University*; James Pressley
198   *Illustration of Judas Maccabaeus (1712)*; Church History Department–Sylvester
199   *Psalm 23 from King James Bible (1611)*; Church History Department–Sylvester
200   *Miles Smith's preface to King James Bible*; Church History Department–Sylvester
201   *Title page of King James Bible (1611)*; Church History Department–Sylvester
202   *Dedication to King James*; Church History Department–Sylvester
203   *Map of Jerusalem from King James Bible (1611)*; Church History Department–Sylvester
208   *King James Bible, scroll, and electronic Bible*; Church History Department–Sylvester
210   *Paul healing the lame man at Lystra*; Church History Department–Sylvester
213   *Julia Smith's Bible*; Church History Department–Sylvester
214   *Four Volumes of Ferrar Fenton's Bible*; Church History Department–Sylvester
215   *The Lord's Prayer in the Chicago Bible*; Church History Department–Sylvester
217   *New English Bible Committee*; The New English Bible. ©1961 Oxford University Press and Cambridge University Press. Reprinted with permission.
218   *Stack of assorted translations of the Bible*; The Christian Science Journal–Linda Payne-Sylvester, photographer
220   *Peter being delivered from prison (1824 English Bible)*; Church History Department–Sylvester